On the Trail of Bears

Dedicated to Mishio Hoshino

English translation © Copyright 1998
by Barron's Educational Series, Inc.
Original edition © 1997 by Edition Nathan, Paris, France
Titre de l'édition originale: *Cap sur les Ours*
publiée par Les Editions Nathan, Paris
French edition by Catherine and Rémy Marion, Illustrations by Jean Chevallier
Graphics and page design by Pierre Dusser, Maps by Noël Blotti

All inquiries should be addressed to:
Barron's Educational Series, Inc.
250 Wireless Boulevard
Hauppauge, NY 11788
http://www.barronseduc.com

Library of Congress Catalog Card No. 98-5829

International Standard Book No. 0-7641-0596-5

Library of Congress Cataloging-in-Publication Data

Marion, Rémy.
 [Cap sur les ours. English]
 On the trail. Bears / Rémy Marion ; illustrations by Jean
Chevallier.
  p. cm.
 Includes bibliographical references and index.
 ISBN 0-7641-0596-5
 1. Bears. I. Chevallier, Jean, artiste. II. Title.
QL737.C27M329713 1998
599.78—dc21   98-5829
                                                   CIP

Printed in Italy
9 8 7 6 5 4 3 2 1

On the Trail of Bears

Catherine and Rémy Marion

Illustrations by Jean Chevallier

BARRON'S
Nature Travel Guides

Table of Contents

7   Foreword

9   **Introducing the Bears**
10   Classification
10   Origin and Evolution
11   Physical Appearance
12   Lifestyle

19   **Bears and Humans**
20   A Family History
21   Hunting Bears

23   **Endangered Bears**
24   Collared Bear or Asiatic Black Bear
26   Sun Bear or Malaysian Bear
28   Sloth Bear
30   Spectacled Bear
32   Giant Panda

35   **American Black Bear**
36   Description...
42   United States (Alaska): Hyder
47   Canada (Manitoba): Riding Mountain National Park
52   United States (Tennessee and North Carolina):
        Great Smoky Mountains National Park

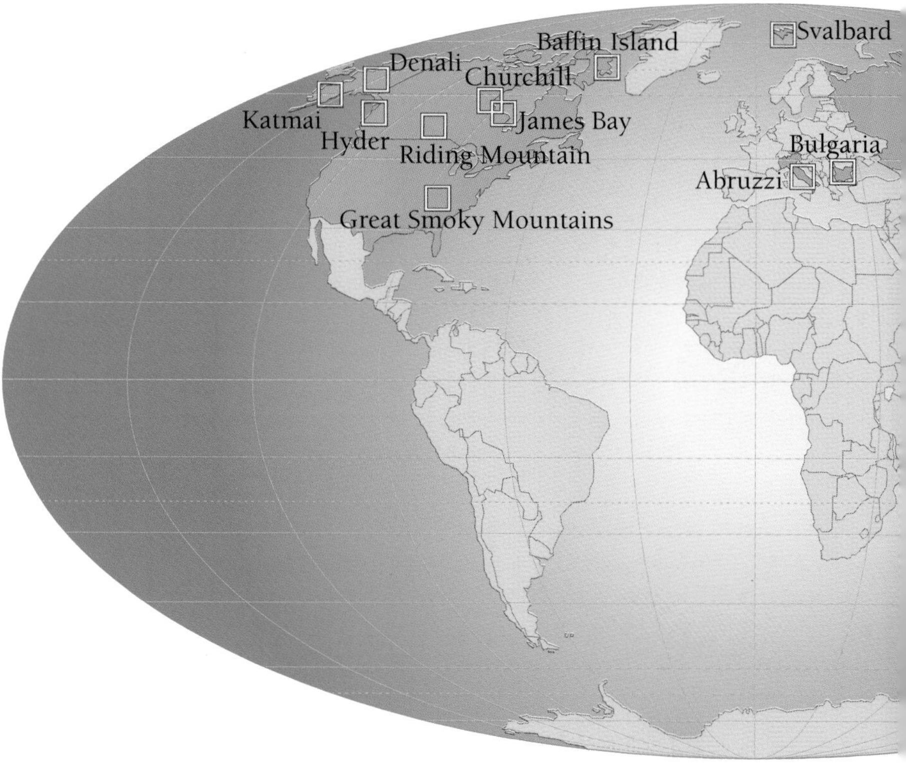

4

Baffin Island   Svalbard
Denali   Churchill
Katmai   James Bay
Hyder   Riding Mountain   Bulgaria
                               Abruzzi
Great Smoky Mountains

57 **Grizzly (Brown) Bear**
58   Description...
64   Italy (Umbria): Abruzzi National Park
69   Bulgaria: In the Heart of the Balkans
73   Russia (Far Eastern Siberia): Magadan Province
78   United States (Alaska): Denali National Park and Preserve
83   United States (Alaska): Katmai National Park

89 **The Polar Bear**
91   Description...
96   Canada (Manitoba): Churchill
101   Canada (Ontario): James Bay
106   Canada (Baffin Island):
      Auyuittuq National Park and Surrounding Areas
111   Norway: Svalbard Archipelago

117 **Appendix**
118   Living with Bears
119   Observing and Photographing Bears
121   Protecting Bears
123   Some Associations and Organizations Involved with Bears
124   Dictionary (French, English, Russian, Norwegian)
125   Glossary
125   Bibliography
127   Indexes

5

Magadan

Foreword

Even the most seasoned naturalist will feel both fear and fascination at the sight of a polar bear in motion, with its supple, elegant gait, or of a grizzly eating. Indeed, observing bears in the wild is one of the most extraordinary experiences that a nature lover can have. This guide describes locations chosen because they offer the chance to watch bears without resorting to the use of bait. Regardless of the site you visit, you are never 100 percent certain that you'll see a bear, but the odds are good at the sites in this guide. They are also places of remarkable natural beauty.

This book is as much about bears as it is about their relationship with humans, who have coexisted with them for centuries. People have, over time, harmed bears and continue to do so, which makes it even more important that they understand the place that the bear occupies in our civilization and the reasons we want to read about it or see it in the wild.

In describing observation sites, this book covers only the most common species available for viewing in the wild. Although we describe the characteristics and habits of, for example, the sloth bear and the spectacled bear, we include no viewing sites. Appropriate sites are difficult to find, and we felt it would be irresponsible to encourage observers, however respectful, to seek these animals when they are already threatened by deforestation and human overpopulation in their native habitat.

This guide provides directions on where and how to observe the most accessible bears in their habitat. It also presents enough information so that you can set off with adequate knowlege of the facts. Keep in mind, however, that nothing can replace personal familiarity with the site or conversations with those in daily contact with the area and the animals that live there.

Off to see the bears!

INTRODUCING THE BEARS

Classification

The bear belongs to the order Carnivora, which includes more than 200 living species. The family of bears, or Ursidae, currently contains eight species distributed in three genera: the giant panda (*Ailuropoda melanoleuca*); the spectacled bear (*Tremarctos ornatus*); the sun bear (*Ursus malayanus*); the sloth bear (*Ursus ursinus*); the American black bear (*Ursus americanus*); the Asian black bear (*Ursus thibetanus*); the grizzly bear (*Ursus arctos*); and the polar bear (*Ursus maritimus*). Fossil analysis has not explained the phylogenic relationships among the species, but their close kinship has been proven genetically. Species boundaries are blurry and somewhat arbitrary. Numerous cases of hybridization have crossed polar bears with grizzly bears or grizzly bears with black bears. The individuals born of these hybridizations in captivity have produced fertile offspring.

10

Origin and evolution

All carnivores have common ancestors, the Miacidae, who lived during the Paleocene epoch, around 40 to 50 million years ago. These small tree-dwelling mammals had a particularly well-developed dental structure with canine teeth for ripping flesh and molars for grinding seeds. Over time, the Miacidae split into two main lines: the arctoides and the aeluroides. From the

Double page preceding. A grizzly bear stands up to be able to better smell the arrival of a female bear with her two cubs. It will flee shortly to avoid contact (Siberia).

When running, bears lift both limbs on the same side at the same time, running in an amble.

former came four large families, the Canidae, Ursidae, Procyonidae, and Mustelidae, and the order of Pinnidia. The latter line differentiated into the Felidae, Hyenidae, Viverridae, and Hespestidae. According to paleontologists, the Ursidae branch became distinct from that of the raccoons (Procyonidae) and the Canidae in the early Miocene period, between 20 and 25 million years ago, in the form of the *Ursavus*, which descended from the cephalogal, a canid of the Oligocene period. The species *Ursavus elmensis*, whose members were no larger than a raccoon, certainly originated from one of two taxa, the first of which was a common origin of all the Ursidae, and the second of which now has no living representatives. The ancestors of the panda differentiated from the branch of the other Ursidae approximately 15 million years ago. The group of short-nosed bears split off between 8 and 10 million years ago; its only surviving species is the spectacled bear that now inhabits northern South America. Other species of short-nosed bears, such as the enormous *Arctodus simus*, still lived on the plains of North America 10,000 years ago.

The first species that showed all the characteristics of the genus *Ursus* developed about 5 million years ago—a small-species bear, *Ursus minimus*. That species then evolved about 2.5 million years ago into *Ursus etruscus*, whose subsequent differentiation concluded, after several intermediate stages about which experts do not agree, into six new species. Of these, the cave bear (*Ursus spelaeus*) disappeared without any descendants about 14,000 years ago.

Analysis of bear DNA yields a picture of the evolution and differentiation of the species. The genus *Ursus* evolved slowly, principally in Eurasia, which is still home to

the largest number of ursine species, but the short-nosed bears spread across all the Americas. Fossil and genetic evidence confirm the close relationship among the grizzly, black, Asiatic black, and polar bears. The polar bear appears to be the most recently differentiated species. It is the result of the evolution of an isolated group, closely related to the grizzly bear. At the time of the Pleistocene glaciations, 150,000 years ago, this group was subjected to extreme climatic conditions that forced them to feed on the only abundant prey, the seal.

In contrast, the evidence does not confirm that the two other Ursidae, the sloth bear and the sun bear, are closely related to other bears. The old classification called these bears, respectively, *Melursus ursinus* and *Helarctos malayanus*. They were reclassified recently and placed in the center of the genus *Ursus*, although little is known about their evolution. Some paleontologists have placed their differentiation in the Pliocene era, between 3 and 10 million years ago.

of various consistencies and so must be able to grind seeds, pine cones, and roots, while retaining the ability to rip the flesh off a piece of carrion. Its dental structure resembles that of a wild boar more than that of a lion. The polar bear, which became a carnivore although it descended from an ancient omnivore, is a unique case in the natural history of animals. Its teeth had to make a reverse journey along the long road of evolution. The polar bear redeveloped the pointed molars that completely disappeared in the grizzly bear, its closest relative.

Bears commonly have a thick fur that both keeps them warm during their hibernation sleep and protects them from the many threats of the forest. They shed every year. In June the grizzly bear's fur begins to regrow on its back, hindquarters, and belly. In August, a new coat starts to appear on the entire body, and by mid-September the animal again is covered with a fur coat capable of protecting it during the winter.

All bears have short tails and nonretractable claws. These claws are usually longer on the front paws than on the hind paws, especially

11

Physical appearance

Bear species differ greatly, and it is quite difficult to describe a typical bear. An adult may weigh as little as 22 pounds (10 kg) (a female sun bear, for example) to as much as 1,540 pounds (700 kg) for a male polar bear. Differences in dental structure show how evolution has affected each bear subspecies. The teeth are adapted for specific food regimens. The grizzly bear, an omnivore, feeds on plants

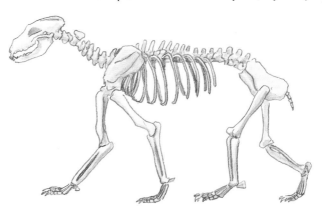

Grizzly bear skeleton.

in species that burrow, such as the grizzly and sloth bears.

Bears, like humans, are plantigrades, which means that, as they move, they place the entire bottom surface of the foot on the ground. In the imprint of the front paws, the palm of the sole makes a deep mark in the soil. The distance between the middle of the balls of the interior and exterior digits provides a good idea of the size of an individual. Bear's soles and toes are heavily padded and covered with a thick, horny leather. While it is soft and flexible, it is almost impossible to cut.

The bears' pace is called an amble; in walking or running they raise both limbs of one side at the same time. Their mode of feeding obliges them to cover a vast amount of territory to find sufficient nourishment. Although they seem to move slowly, they in fact cover forest, marsh, and mountains at a constant and relatively swift pace, crossing passes at altitudes exceeding 13,120 feet (4,000 m). Despite their bulk, grizzlies can sprint as fast as 35 mph (56 km per hour).

Lakes and sea inlets are not obstacles to their progress. Bears are good swimmers, and they enjoy bathing. Bears, even grizzly bears that weigh more than 550 pounds (250 kg), retained their early ancestors' great agility in climbing trees. The sun bear, which is almost totally tree-dwelling, builds a nest of leaves and branches where it rests and eats.

Whether bears inhabit closed ecosystems such as forest or bush-covered terrain or vast open spaces such as ice floes, they have developed the same sensory capabilities. Their vision can be compared to that of humans. In general they make little sound except during the reproductive period and for communication between the young and mothers.

Bears' sense of smell is quite strong. In an open environment, across several yards of undergrowth or hundreds of miles of ice, this sense permits the bears to find a partner, detect carrion, or identify danger. When an odor interests them, bears rise up to sniff better. A polar bear can smell a seal more than 20 miles (32 km) away.

Bear's eyes are forward facing, like humans. Their ability to discern shape and color recognition is excellent. Their hearing is also quite good; they can pick up sounds of normal human conversation over a distance of 1/4 mile away.

12

Lifestyle

Winter hibernation

Bears hibernate in their own fashion, distinct from that of rodents. With winter's arrival, rodents fall into a state in which their body temperature drops by several degrees. In spring, they need several days to emerge from this state. Bears, in contrast, maintain an internal temperature four to five degrees lower than normal during their winter sleep. If a mild period occurs, they can emerge from their den. In their sleepy state, they require less nourishment. If food remains abundant during winter, as on ice floes, bears, except for pregnant females, remain active.

Polar bears generally do not hibernate; only the females preparing to give birth enclose themselves in a den beginning in October. The Asiatic black bear also does not hibernate except for those that inhabit the northern part of its range. It does spend short periods in a den in the southern zone if weather conditions are especially harsh.

For the grizzly bears, the period of hibernation may last from one to seven months, depending on the climate. During this period, the bears neither feed, drink, nor excrete waste. They don't need to drink all winter because water is produced when their fat calories are burned. Thus, in autumn, they must store large reserves of fat by ingesting up to 20,000 calories per day of fruit, acorns, berries, and beechnuts. The hibernating metabolism of the bear is a unique phenomenon among mammals. Nitrogenous waste produced in the transformation of fat into energy is recycled into new reserves. The oxygenation of bears' blood is also transformed: in its prolonged domant state, the grizzly bear, for example, has a heartbeat reduced to less than ten per minute (compared with fifty during rest in its active state). To accommodate this drastic decrease in the circulation of blood within the organism, only the vital tissues and organs receive the normal quantity of oxygenated blood.

In the den, a full-grown bear burns about 4,000 calories each day. That means it loses around eight pounds every week while hibernating.

For the female bear, winter is the period of giving birth; she has to nurse her cubs using her fat reserves. The den under a stump or in a cave is the ideal shelter during this critical period.

13

All grizzly bears spend the winter in a den, but they come out occasionally in January if there is a warm spell.

Social life

Bears tend to be solitary, rather than social, animals. Their interaction is limited to gatherings at points of abundant food, the family living space (established by the female and her young), and encounters during the mating season, however, exceptions to this exist. The sun bear does live in couples. The sloth bear, which is the most social, communicates with facial expressions and a large variety of sonorous vocalizations that are more developed than those in other species.

In areas where food is abundant, more than 20 bears may fish only a few meters apart, observing a strict hierachy in which the large males occupy the choicest spots. The bears establish these relations through a combination of postures and behaviors whose purpose is to limit clashes. A bear signals that its neighbor has come too close by opening its jaws wide; an inferior shows humility to a dominant individual by lowering its head toward the ground and withdrawing.

A whale carcass may attract several dozen polar bears who stand shoulder to shoulder when they come to tear up the fat flesh. Around the Churchill region, several dozen bears may be seen side by side without having particularly abundant food to share.

Reproduction

Bears of reproductive age (which varies by species) in the Northern Hemisphere are in heat from May to July. Available females emit an unmistakable olfactory trail for potential mates. However, with 50 to 70 percent fewer females than males, the males must fight to transmit their genes. The males' behavior sets off the females' ovulation; the males become irritable, tearing up trees and stumps and flattening bushes. This pattern ensures the best chances for successful fertilization.

The couple remains together for a few days, copulating numerous times. After this period, the two partners separate and feed copiously. The female may well find a second partner. The egg is not implanted in the uterus immediately after fertilization, but only at the end of several months; this is called delayed implantation. This mechanism

14

At a place rich in salmon, individual bears must assert their dominance. Gaining the best spot ensures a huge quantity of fish for a minimum effort (Alaska).

In a Finnish forest in early summer, male and female meet at a quiet spot and spend some time together.

is necessary to the survival of bears that live in cold regions. The bears usually mate in spring. If the embryo developed immediately after copulation, the young would be born in autumn, a cold time when nourishment is sparse. Because of the delay, birth occurs in midwinter, in the maternal den. The young do not emerge from the den until spring, the most favorable time of year for survival. Although this process is less important in tropical regions, it nevertheless continues in all the bear species, with the possible exception of the spectacled bear.

Birth takes place in a cave, among roots or beneath a thick layer of vegetation. The female gives birth to one to three cubs, with two the most common number. The newborns are tiny and delicate. A newborn Malay cub weighs no more than 7 1/2 pounds (325 g); its smooth skin is covered with a fine down.

Feeding

The majority of carnivores, such as large cats, feed themselves every two or three days, ingesting as much meat as possible at that time.

Bears, unlike other carnivores, must spend long hours seeking their food, which consists mainly of plants. Because this diet is low in protein, the bears must consume large quantities of food. Feeding regiments vary according to species. Some bears have highly specialized diets, such as the giant panda, which eats almost nothing other than bamboo, and the sloth bear, which eats little other than termites and ants. The polar bear is the most carnivorous of the family and the only large predator. The other species are predominantly omnivorous, with plant consumption dominating. Specific adaptations have enabled them to take advantage of available food sources that

16

Grizzly bears are mainly vegetarians; when the grass is tender, they take delight in it and graze for the entire day.

other animals have exploited little or not at all. In temperate regions, the ability to cover a large territory allows each individual access to varied resources every year. As it travels, the bear is able to feed on plants, invertebrates, carion, and even mammals and birds. In tropical regions, bears can remain in one place for several days and consume all the available nourishment: fruits, leaves, worms, and insects.

The spectacled bear, for example, eats some plant species such as the leaves and nuts of palm trees, cactus, orchids, and various bromeliads. When the sloth bear has located a termite nest, it digs an opening in it with its large claws. It places its long snout at the entrance of this hole and blows violently to remove dust and dirt. It recloses its nostrils in order not to swallow the dust, then, with a powerful inhalation, it swallows the insects. The structure of its palate, its mobile lips, and the cavity formed by its two missing upper incisors act like a household vacuum cleaner.

Bears are also fond of honey and will rip apart beehives or the nests of wild bees to get it. Their long, thick fur helps shield them from bee stings.

Humans' relationship with bears has always been ambiguous, a mixture of fear, hatred, and admiration. Living on the same land does not necessarily improve the situation between the two populations. Some bears take advantage of the proximity of humans to feed at their expense; cornfields in the foothills of the Andes for the spectacled bear, livestock in northern India for the Asiatic black bear, and orchards in Manitoba for the black bear. Dumping grounds also attract opportunistic animals who sometimes find easily digested, cooked food in trash receptacles.

Life expectancy

The life span of an individual bear varies according to the constraints to which it is exposed. Although large adult bears have no predators, smaller bears must fear the puma, jaguar, or leopard. Wolves occasionally attack young black and polar bears.

Bears harbor numerous internal parasites, of which more than 50 have been identified and described. They suffer from diseases similar to those that afflict humans, such as arthritis, tuberculosis, and bronchial pneumonia. They have numerous dental problems, especially the males, whose teeth may be broken or pulled out during the combat of the mating season. Often the snout, the shoulders, and the flanks of a bear are encircled with deep scars.

17

The young bear never leaves its mother, especially when taking a nap. If left alone, it becomes the prey of an adult male (Canada).

BEARS AND HUMANS

A family history

Over thousands of years, bears and humans have shared shelter and nutritional resources. As the two species alternately preyed on and hunted each other, their relations were equalized. Man found in the bear his wild twin; the old adage says, "Skin a bear and you will find a man." Indeed, the skinned body of a bear has a strange resemblance to that of a human. Numerous other similarities link the two species: erect posture, suckling in a seated position, and an omnivorous feeding regimen, among others. The annual rhythm of bears' lives, determined by the seasons, is close to that of the Native Americans, Inuit, or Sames: a winter of torpor in the shelter of a cabin or an igloo, a spring of light and deliverance, a summer devoted to reproductive activities, an autumn of abundant feeding, and uncertainty about the coming winter. In the spring, Native Americans viewed the return of the bears as a good omen, like the return of a relative and a sign of rejuvenation. It was and still is celebrated by feasts in many countries, in the Andes and the Pyrenees, as well as in the Carpathians and on Sakhalin Island. During raucous carnivals, men give full vent to their madness. One or several boys dressed as bears, liberated from their human constraints, pursue young women and insult the onlookers. The dance of the bears

20

Double page preceding. In Siberia, grizzly bears and salmon fishermen come into contact as they share space in the summer, the fish season.

For many years, the bears of Yellowstone Park have fed on the garbage left by man, reaching the point that virtual shows resulted at places where trash containers were dumped.

4261. Brown Bear Waiting for Garbage, Yellowstone National Park

is found everywhere in the world. In North America, hundreds of such dances exist. They mark the change of the seasons or the harvest, they help humans prepare for war or for hunting bears, they are connected with certain rites of initiation, or they give homage to the bear emerging from its den. All these dances, primordial expressions of the cult of the bear, are the occasion for large demonstrations that bring several villages together. In the eastern part of the continent, where the grizzly does not exist, the dancers imitate the less menacing, calmer black bear with less violent imitations.

The bear occupies a unique place in the imagination of world civilizations. All the peoples of the Northern Hemisphere have stories and legends in which the bear is the central character. The bear mythology of many cultures—the Greeks, the Inuit of Greenland, the Sames of Finland, and the Cree of James Bay in Canada, for example—contains many themes; the myths and their analysis would fill dozens of volumes.

For the Native Americans of the northwest coast of America, the bear is the original mother of the people. The doors of the community houses symbolize the birth canal of the bear.

For the Sames, the bear was an ancestor gifted with as much intelligence as humans and possessing the strength of nine or ten men.

For the Ainu of Japan or the Inuit of Baffin Island, a man or a woman could establish a household and produce a family with a female or a male bear. Since prehistoric times, from the caves of Vercors to the tundra of the Taymyr Peninsula in Siberia, men have raised pillars to exhibit the skulls of bears, arranged in a circle of placed on posts. The meaning of such monuments remains unknown.

Among peoples who hunted bears, the hunt was guided by a strict protocol, which the hunters had to respect at the risk of returning empty-handed or being attacked by the animal. One had to ask the bear's forgiveness before killing it and gain a state of grace so that the bear would let its fellow creatures know of the welcome that humans had in store for it. Gifts were offered at the skinning in a ceremony with strict taboos, identical to those established for the death of a member of the family.

Many examples illustrate the ambiguity of modern relations between humans and bears. Marcel Couturier, a renowned scholar of bears, hunted bears in the Pyrenees while at the same time regretting bitterly their increasing scarcity! At the beginning of the century, the Duke of Orleans, after himself bagging dozens of polar bears, deplored the slaughter perpetrated by poor half-trappers, half-hermits. In 1903 Theodore Roosevelt, the great bear hunter, became the godfather of the famous teddy bear when he refused to kill a bear cub during a hunting expedition. Since that time, teddy bears made of straw or fluff have comforted and consoled many small children.

Hunting bears

People have hunted bears as long as the two groups have occupied the same territory. In the beginning, armed only with flint, they could not risk direct combat, so they trapped bears in trenches. With bows and spears, they could wound the bear, then kill it while remaining outside the range of its dangerous claws. Depending on the region, hunters attacked fattened individuals for their thick fur. In winter, they attacked sleeping bears deep in their dens. The Inuit have hunted the polar bears this way for thousands of years, armed with only a bone- or ivory-tipped weapon. Dogs were precious helpers because they could sniff out a den camouflaged under the snow. They were first trained to defend hunters against bears, then for hunting. Since the Middle Ages, the bear has been the game of royalty. From Charlemagne to Charles XII of Sweden, kings went into direct combat against a bear armed with a dagger or a pitchfork.

Later, large landowners saw the bear as an obstacle to the clearing of land for agriculture. The landowners offered prizes for killing bears, and bear products were offered for sale: pelts, fat, and meat. Some parts of the bear became known for their pharmaceutical or culinary qualities. Thus, the bear became a source of profit. The Hudson's Bay Company, which began fur trading with the Native Americans toward the end of the seventeenth century, encouraged trappers to trade pelts for goods.

They exchanged the warm black-bear pelts for wool blankets. The animal respected and deified by the Native Americans became an exchange currency.

Demographic expansion of the human race has restricted the bear's habitat and changed its behavior accordingly. Sheep and cattle came to the edge of the forests to graze. Beehives were established, and fields of corn replaced the moist prairies. For a bear, what could be more tempting than to kill a sheep or to pillage a hive full of honey? The bear thus became a "nuisance." Villagers of India, Peru, and the Pyrenees organized slaughters officially sanctioned by village elders. The bear had no chance against an army of villagers anxious to participate in eradicating a blood-thirsty beast. The skinned carcass was exhibited on a frame in the center of the village. Numerous types of bear-catching devices were invented: traps, nooses, clubs, and trenches bristling with spikes. In some regions, even poison—strychnine—was used.

Subsequently, bear hunts underwent changes in both style and method. With the advent of guns, some bear hunts became veritable massacres. Some hunters initially continued to prefer the spear, which was more trustworthy than primitive firearms, but very soon humans were reassured about the reliability of guns. By the end of the nineteenth century, bear hunting had become fashionable among certain groups. Hunters who had never seen a bear nevertheless set out across the world to kill one. Immediately after World War II, the practice of hunters chartering helicopters to kill polar bears began. This hastened the decline of the population and made the species even rarer.

21

Hunting at bear dens is still in practice in some parts of Russia.

ENDANGERED BEARS

Collared bear or Asiatic black bear

(Ursus thibetanus)

OTHER NAMES: Himalayan black bear, Tibetan black bear.

Average length: 51–74 inches (130–190 cm).

Weight: Adult male, 220–440 pounds (100–200 kg); adult female, 100–275 pounds (50–125 kg); newborn, 27–105 ounces (77–300 g).

Description: Often called the collared bear because of the white crescent adorning its chest. This marking varies in distinctness and size and may even be completely absent. Aside from that marking, the animal resembles a smaller version of its cousin, the American black bear. Its thick fur is most often completely black; sometimes it is dark brown.

24

Habitat: Inhabits forests in mountainous regions. It is found at elevations up to 9,840 feet (3000 m), and it winters in valleys. An adult occupies a territory of 2.7–3 square miles (7–8 square km). The bears inhabiting the northern part of its range hibernate, but those in the south do not; climatic conditions are milder. The Asiatic black bear is distinctly nocturnal; during the day it sleeps in trees or in caves.

Food: It feeds on fruits, the nests of bees, insects, invertebrates, small vertebrates, and carrion; more rarely it attacks domestic animals.

Maturity: Females reach maturity between three and four years of age.

Reproduction: In Russia mating occurs in June and July, and birth takes place between December and March. In Pakistan these events occur in October and February, respectively.

Predation: The young may be prey for grizzly bears.

Range: The Asiatic black bear has a wide range. It is found in Iran, Afghanistan, northern Pakistan, the eastern Himalayas, and in the Tibetan Plateau, which extends to Manchuria in the north, to the forests of China. Burma and Laos are the limit of its range on the Asian continent. The bear also is found on the Japanese islands of Honshu and Shikoku and as far as Taiwan.

Population: Unknown.

History: The victim of poaching and deforestation, the Asiatic black bear has an uncertain future. Several have been captured for training and exhibition in the markets of northern India.

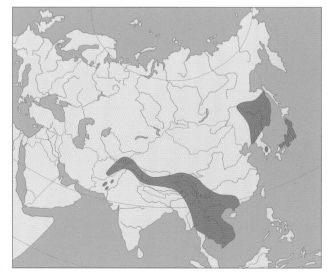

Double page preceding. A rare photo of an Asiatic black bear in the wild, here at an especially inhospitable location that is one of their last refuges far from the pressure of human civilization.

Sun bear or Malaysian bear

(Ursus malayanus)

Average length: 47–58 1/2 inches (120–150 cm). The smallest of the bears.

Shoulder height: 27 inches (70 cm).

Weight: Adult, 59–143 pounds (27–65 kg) (the male is 10 to 20 percent heavier than the female); newborn, 79–114 ounces (225–325 g).

Description: Dull fur consists of short strands that give it a sleek appearance. Its forehead is furrowed and looks wrinkled. Its muzzle is shortened and has an orange coloring that extends to below the eyes. The chest is marked with a yellowish-white collar whose form varies. The paws have long, curved claws that are particularly adapted for tree climbing. The sun bear is also known as the "honey bear" because it has a particular fondness for that food, and as the Malayan bear because of its range. In Thailand it is also called the "bear dog" because it is not much bigger than a large dog. Its English name, sun bear, reflects the crescent-shaped spot on its chest, a symbol of the rising sun in Asiatic folklore. This marking varies in size and shape in different individuals and is occasionally absent.

Habitat: The sun bear is limited to humid tropical forests at low altitude. It rests and feeds in trees but travels on the ground.

Food: Its diet is diverse and includes termites, small mammals, birds, and bee nests. The bear also eats young palm plants in plantations and climbs trees to take honey from hives. Its habits are mainly nocturnal.

Maturity: Females reach maturity in their third year.

Reproduction: The mating period, which lasts only from two to seven days, may occur at any time during the year, as may birth. Gestation is 100 days.

Range: Its range extends from northeastern India— where it was rediscovered in the 1980s—to Bangladesh, southern China, Burma, Thailand, Cambodia, Vietnam, and the islands of Java, Sumatra, and Borneo.

Population: Unknown.

History: Because of habitat destruction and poaching, the sun bear has become rare in the northern and western parts of its range.

26

Sloth bear
(Ursus ursinus)

Average length: 55–74 inches (140–190 cm).

Shoulder height: 33 inches (85 cm).

Weight: Adult male, 176–310 pounds (80–140 kg); adult female, 121–209 pounds (55–95 kg); newborn, 105–175 ounces (300–500 g).

Description: The sloth bear is also called the thick-lipped bear because of its thick lower lip, whose long, mobile structure enables it to catch the insects and larvae that are its main food. Its hair is black and shaggy, with particularly long strands on the shoulders. The chest is marked with a large U or Y. The muzzle and eye area are of a light color. The tail, longer than that of other species, measures 6 1/4 inches (16–18 cm). Various explanations are given for the origin of its name. One is that the tousled, abundant hair, the long, inwardly curved claws, and the habit of hanging from tree branches gave early observers the impression that the bear was related to the South American sloth. Another explanation links the name exclusively to the similar claws; eighteenth-century observers called it the "Ursine Bradypus" and named it *Bradypus ursinus* for the New World sloths (*Bradypus*). However, despite the resemblance, this is definitely a bear, as the current Latin name indicates: *Ursus ursinus*, the bearlike bear.

28

Habitat: The sloth bear inhabits forested regions and woodlands at low altitudes and seems to occupy a limited territory. Deforestation continues to reduce its habitat.

Food: The diet essentially consists of termites. The sloth bear appears to have adapted to this specialized diet in several ways: the disappearance of two upper incisors to improve breathing and extended lips to snatch up insects. This food is supplemented with eggs, berries, sugarcane, corn, and carrion. The bear feeds mainly at night.

Mortality: The young remain with their mother until they are two or three years old, and all tolerate the male's presence. This extended period makes it likely that fewer of these bears die in the first years.

Maturity: It is not known at what age these bears reach maturity.

Reproduction: Mating occurs from May to July, except in Sri Lanka where it continues year-round. Gestation is six to seven months with delayed fertilization. The young are born in the dry season.

Range: The sloth bear is found mainly in Sri Lanka and India, but it also lives in Bangladesh, Bhutan, and Nepal. Although some live at the base of the Himalayas, the species is not likely to occupy the same territory as the Asiatic black bear.

Population: Its population is declining steadily and is estimated at between seven thousand and ten thousand individuals.

History: The bears were used in circuses and called the juggling bear.

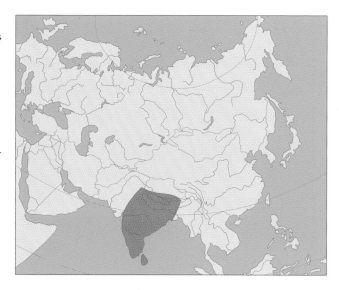

Spectacled bear

(Tremarctos ornatus)

OTHER NAMES: Short-faced bear, Andean bear, or "ucumari."

Average length: 55–74 inches (140–190 cm).

Shoulder height: 29 3/4 inches (76 cm).

Weight: Adult male, 220–340 pounds (100–155 kg), (maximum 385 pounds, 175 kg); adult female, 141–180 pounds (64–82 kg); newborn, 105–175 ounces (300–500 g).

Description: The spectacled bear is dull colored and small and is distinguishable by the cream-colored circles around the eyes, which may extend to the throat and chest. The species' name, *ornatus,* meaning decorated, refers to these circles. The bear's claws are specially adapted for climbing trees.

Habitat: The spectacled bear frequents forests of all types, humid and dry, as well as steppes. With habitat loss, it takes refuge in dense, humid forests at high altitude 5,900–8,900 feet (1,800–2,700 m).

Food: Diet consists primarily of berries, grasses, sugarcane, and corn. Less than 5 percent of its diet is made up of mammals, including rabbits and rodents, and birds. It consumes 22 species of bromeliads, 11 species of cactus, 32 different fruits, and 10 other plants, including orchid bulbs. To reach fruit it wants to eat, the bear can climb as high as 49 feet (15 m) and remain for three or four days in the same tree. The timid spectacled bear feeds at dawn and twilight. Its feeding habits aid forest regeneration because it disperses seeds.

Longevity: Twenty-five years or more.

Maturity: Females reach maturity between four and seven years of age.

Reproduction: Mating occurs between April and June. Partners remain together for one or two weeks, copulating frequently. Gestation lasts from five and a half to eight months. Between November and February, the female gives birth, usually to two, but sometimes to three, young.

Range: The spectacled bear is found in the Andes on both sides of the equator. Known also as the Andean bear, its habitat extends northward into Venezuela and southward across Colombia, Ecuador, Peru, and Bolivia, and even into Chile. Some have said that the bear is found as far north as Panama and as far south as Argentina, but no recent observation has confirmed this.

Population: The species is endangered, with about 2,000 individuals remaining in the wild. The decline was caused by the intensive deforestation that accompanies agriculture.

History: The existence of the spectacled bear became known to Europeans at the beginning of the nineteenth century, when a specimen was captured in Chile and brought to England. The spectacled bear is the second-largest mammal in South America, the rarest of the bear species, and the only species belonging to the genus *Tremarctos.*

Giant panda

(Ailuropoda melanoleuca)

CHINESE NAME: Xiongmao (giant bear cat).

Average length: 62–74 inches (160–190 cm).

Weight: Adult male, 187–275 pounds (85–125 kg); adult female, 154–220 pounds (70–100 kg); newborn, 5 ounces (140 g).

Description: The giant panda's coat is very recognizable: the body is white, and the paws, ears, and the area surrounding the eyes are black. The head is masive compared with the rest of the body. The forepaws have six digits; the sixth is actually an elongated wrist bone. The stomach is adapted for the digestion of bamboo. The fur, oily and thick, serves as protection from moisture.

Habitat and movement: The giant panda lives at altitudes of 3,900–11,500 feet (1,200–3,500 m) in dense bamboo forests. Average territory for an individual is 3.2 square miles (8.5 square km) for a male and 1.8 square miles (4.6 square km) for a female.

Food: 99 percent of its diet consists of the leaves, shoots, and branches of bamboo, of which there are 30 types. An adult requires 26–33 pounds (12–15 kg) of bamboo per day generally, and 84 pounds (38 kg) when the bamboo is green. Occasionally other plants and meat supplement this very specific diet. The animal is active mainly at night.

Longevity: The panda lives for more than twenty years in captivity, and its life-span exceeds twenty-five years in the wild.

Maturity: The panda reaches maturity between 4 1/2 and 6 1/2 years.

Reproduction: Mating occurs between March and May, birth between August and September. The females raise only one young at a time, which stays with them for a period of eighteen months.

Range: The small remaining population lives in six isolated zones in southwestern China (all in the provinces of Sichuan, Gansu, and Shaanxi). The population occupies a total area of about 5,320 square miles (14,000 square km).

Population: Between 700 to 1,000 individuals remain in the wild.

History: For centuries the panda was considered the domestic animal of the Chinese emperors. Europeans first encountered it in 1869, when a French missionary gave a skin to the Museum of Natural History in Paris.

Since then, the animal has suffered the full force of the population expansion in China and is now considered one of the rarest species in the world. Although the Communist government gave it the status of "national treasure," this did not halt the decline of the panda population. The clearing of bamboo forests, its only source of nourishment, is the main reason for the decline of the panda population, although poaching has accellerated the process.

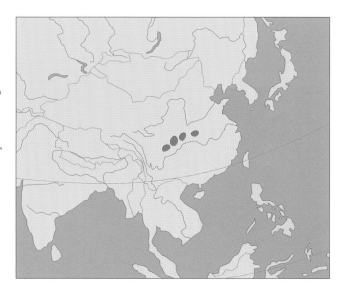

32

Double page following. This young black bear, about two years old, has likely just left its mother; famished, it has come to feed at a campsite (Canada).

American
Black
Bear

(Ursus americanus)

Description

Average length: Adult, 58 1/2–78 inches (150–200 cm).
Shoulder height: 35–39 inches (90–100 cm).
Weight: male, 264–594 pounds (120–270 kg) (maximum recorded weight at Riding Mountain National Park in Manitoba is 803 pounds, 365 kg); female, 165–264 pounds (75–120 kg); newborn, 122 ounces (350 g). 4 1/2–8 1/2 pounds (2–4 kg) upon leaving the den for the first time.

The bears' coat is most often black but the shade may vary from chocolate to cinnamon, with brown an intermediate color. It can even be white; in this case, it is called a spirit bear, or Kermoda bear. The coat also may verge on a silvery blue-gray. Sometimes lighter bands of color extend along the median line of the back. The muzzle is chestnut. Black bears are characterized by a rectilinear posture and pointed muzzle; the nostrils are elongated, the ears rounded. The imprint of the short claws is not always visible in the bear's footprint.

Habitat

The black bear inhabits all forested zones with clearings, terrain with dense vegetation, steep inclines, seacoasts, and the banks of rivers and streams, as well as the tundra of Labrador. The bear is present only when food is abundant. It avoids clearcut regions within managed forests.

Range

A female covers an area of 2.5–10 square miles (6.5–26 square km). The male covers 7.5–38 square miles (20–100 square km), two to four times that of the female. Territory consists of one zone inhabited exclusively by the individual and another that is shared with other bears.

This territory of the adult male is contiguous with that of several females. A group requires a surface area of 75–171 square miles (200–450 square km).

Food

The black bear is perhaps the most opportunistic species, which certainly explains its great capacity to live in many environments and in proximity to humans. Seventy-five percent of its diet is plants, but the percentage varies according to season and location. In spring, the diet is composed of herbaceous plants, leaves, insects (ants and beetles), fawns (rarely), and beavers; in summer, salmon, crabs, roots, cherries, berries, and wasps (rarely); in autumn, acorns, nuts, carrion, and, at the end of the season, apples. The black bear uses the coolest hours of the day to feed (morning and evening), remaining under the forest cover during the day.

Some populations visit dumping grounds regularly. They have become so

36

The black bears prefer closed areas, steep river banks, and leafy forests, habitats that they share with the red fox, the grouse, and the belted kingfisher.

acclimated to humans that they will remain within several yards of people who have come to dump their garbage.

blue-gray color is found only in the region of Glacier Bay in Alaska. The Kermoda bear is found in two distinct zones: Royal Princess Island north of Vancouver Island and the Terrace region of British Columbia.

Predators

The wolf, the puma, the lynx, feral domestic dogs, and especially humans.

Longevity

They may reach or exceed twenty-five years of age. Among young bears, a major cause of death is premature separation from the mother, to which they must remain close throughout their first year. If they become separated, for example, while crossing a highway, the young starve. The young are also sometimes attacked by large male bears. Once they reach adulthood, the bears face few threats.

Maturity

Females reach maturity at two or three years, after which they may mate under favorable conditions. Males are mature at two years, but only a dominant male can mate with a female.

Range

The black bear lives only in North America and ranges from New Brunswick to Alaska. It is present in 32 of the United States, 5 states of Mexico, and throughout Canada, except for Prince Edward Island. The silvery

38

Less frequently than the grizzly bear, black bears fish for salmon with great efficiency. Their technique is different: they kill the fish immediately and do not return into the water. Then they go out of sight to eat their fish.

Population

The total population, which is increasing, is estimated at between four hundred thousand and seven hundred fifty thousand.

History

Before the arrival of Europeans, and especially before the establishment of the trading posts of the Hudson's Bay Company at the end of the seventeenth century, the black bear was undoubtedly very numerous. Native peoples hunted the bear, which they attacked especially during its winter hibernation. They ate its meat, dressed themselves in its fur, and used its fat as fuel for their lamps. A necklace of bear claws was believed to give strength and courage to warriors. Native Americans sought out the plants that the bear ate in order to attain the same characteristics as the animal. The common names of certain plants illustrate this custom: bear berry (*Arctostaphalos uva-ursi*), bear garlic (*Allium ursinum*), and bear grass (*Xerophyllum tenax*).

The Native Americans never uttered the true name of the bear. The Cree called it "short tail," "the quick-tempered one," or "the one with the chin"; the Koyukon of Alaska called it "the black place," "the dark one," or simply "the animal." The bear was at the center of numerous cults and was the object of profound respect. Natives were fascinated by the many characteristics they had in common with the bear: identical vertical posture and a similar skeleton, especially around the paws, and similar diet.

A hunter had to ask for forgiveness before killing a bear; failure to respect this rule meant that the dead bear's soul would be reincarnated in another bear, which would flee from men, making their hunt fruitless.

The presence of the black bear was felt everywhere: in totemic portrayals, in imitation dances. Places where the bear had appeared, like a symbolic vision of power, became sacred. With colonization, hunting of the bear intensified: over a period of 150 years, the records of the Hudson's Bay

39

In September the black bears look for acorns, apples in orchards, or raspberries in forest clearings.

Company show an average annual export of 9,000 skins. Thousands of skins are still used to make the famous hats worn by the British Palace Guard.

Today, the bears are still hunted in many places, especially in preserves where the population is managed like livestock. The black bear is also the object of very active poaching; some parts of its body, such as the paws and the bile, are sent to Asian pharmacies for their alleged curative powers. In January of 1996, an international plan was finally put in place in Canada to end the international hunting of the black bear.

Annual life cycle

All black bears spend the winter in a den (a hollow tree, cave, or space below collapsed earth, in a nest of leaves and branches) which they use for multiple years. They also may establish themselves in a pile of wood at the end of the garden of an inhabited house.

In northern regions, they return to the den with the first snowfall. They emerge only in spring, after four to seven months of slumber, depending on the latitude. If the temperature is mild enough and the period without food is of short-enough duration, they may not hibernate. In this case they find a shelter to use for short periods. During hibernation, the black bear

does not eat. The heartbeat drops from an average of 50 to 12 beats per minute. No excrement soils the den: the species has developed a system of recycling urine into proteins. The hibernation sleep permits pregnant females to produce between two and five young. Blind and hairless, the cubs spend the winter buried in the thick fur of their mother, consuming rich milk with a 20-percent fat content. When they awaken, the females have lost as much as 40 percent of their weight.

Most individuals leave the den between April and May, with the males exiting first. The exterior temperature, the age of the individual, and its quantity of food reserves determine the time of emergence. Females then live in forests, where the trees shelter their offspring. The young remain with them for at least one year, or even two; they are weaned between July and September of the first year.

Mating season runs from the beginning of June to the beginning of August. Beginning in July, some individuals move to salmon-rich rivers in the west.

The areas of abundant food, where each individual can provide for itself, attracts relatively significant groups—as many as fifteen individuals—for a species that normally is solitary. At such sites it is also possible to see grizzly and black bears together, or even, as was the case in Labrador a few years ago, polar bears and black bears. The most important movements occur at the end of summer and in the beginning of the autumn, when the bear stores the

40

When still quite young, black bears have the habit of hiding in trees. As adults they still can climb up easily to gather acorns (United States).

indispensable fat reserves for its hibernation sleep. During this time, it may consume as many as 20,000 calories per day and grow by as much as 31 pounds (14 kg) per week.

Indications of presence

The black bear inhabits an environment of dense vegetation, moves without making a sound, and avoids contact. To learn its habits, the best strategy is to locate and identify signs of its presence. With vigilance and persistence, one may obtain a

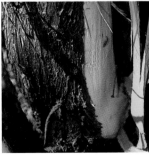

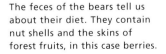

The feces of the bears tell us about their diet. They contain nut shells and the skins of forest fruits, in this case berries.

Scratch marks on the trees show the passage of a bear, but there is nothing to indicate that it has marked a specific territory.

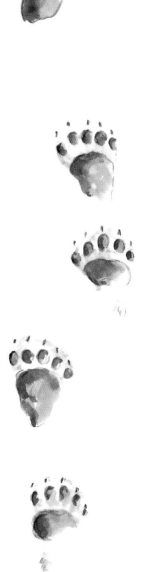

good deal of information, beginning by following the tracks the bear makes in the forest. Its footprints (showing five distinct and parallel toes) are very recognizable. The prints of the front paws measure from 5 to 7 inches (13 to 18 cm) long and from 3 to 4 inches (8 to 10 cm) wide. They show the inwardly curved shape of the toes (for climbing trees), which are separated from each other. The print of the forepaw is found just ahead of that of the hind paw. In mating season and when the bears are shedding, the presence of the bear is indicated by claw marks on the bark of trees, which mark the bear's territory. In some cases, conifers are stripped as the bears remove the bark to feed from the cambium beneath.

In summer and autumn, black bears have an insatiable appetite, and they leave ample feces. These contain undigested materials (nutshells, seeds, fish bones, hair) that permit identification of the animal's diet. At the foot of large trees, a pile of leaves or pine needles with hair adhering to them indicates that a bear has rested there recently.

Broken branches of fruit trees and trampled bushes in areas where berries are abundant also show that a bear has passed through; as it strives to eat as much as possible, the bear is not at all cautious. A carcass with which only turned-out skin remains or an anthill pushed down to the ground are other signs of the bear's presence and indicate the urgency with which it sets about eating.

41

Observation site

United States (Alaska): Hyder

Hyder is located in the Misty Fjords Natural Area, which is part of the Tongass National Forest, established in 1907. Tongass encompasses the entire southeastern fringe of the state of Alaska. Concealed at the end of the Portland Canal, which actually is a fjord 72 miles (116 km) long, Hyder is the southernmost town in Alaska. It is accessible only by road through Stewart, in British Columbia. Because of the forest, the irregular coastline, and the many small islands, one can move around the region only by boat or seaplane. Seaplanes are also used by the U.S. Forest Service, which maintains observation cabins in the area.

Only in 1896 was the Portland Canal explored by Captain D. D. Gaillard for the U.S. Army Corps of Engineers. At about the same time, gold and silver were discovered in the hills around Hyder. Many prospectors moved in and, in 1917, veins of silver were identified in the upper basin of the Salmon River. Hyder was thus developed and became a point of access to and a supply center for the mines. Most mining activity ended in 1956, except for a copper mine that closed in 1984. Today the local economy is based on local trade and tourism. The spectacular terrain has been marked distinctly by glaciers: rivers of ice streaked by moraines and torrents that gush across valleys surrounded by steep hills. At Marks and Fish Creeks, the substrate is typical of terrain drained by glaciers: fine sand, pebbles, and polished rocks. To preserve wildlife, the region between the Fish Creek Bridge and Riverside Mine has been closed to hunting since 1988. The U.S. Forest Service and the Alaska Department of Fish and Game are studying the region to determine how best to promote a friendly and secure environment for both bears and humans.

42

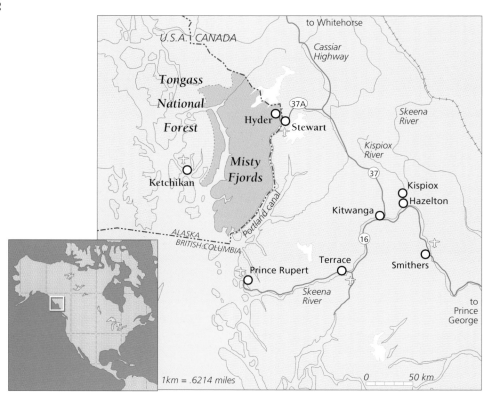

1km = .6214 miles

Fauna and flora

Watering places attract a variety of animals. Silvery seagulls (Mew gulls) assemble near the shore where bears have eaten to consume what the bears left behind. On Moose Pond, Canada geese, various species of ducks, and passerine birds gather. Belted kingfishers, with a characteristic steel-blue color when in flight, like to perch near a pond (the Blue Lagoon) on the other side of the river to hunt for fish. The American dipper also frequents this location. At the bottom of the large pond, beavers have built a lodge, and their dams have increased the area of the waters of Moose Pond. Sometimes a bald eagle comes to perch in the top of

The belted kingfisher is seen frequently on the shore of the Blue Lagoon. It fishes by diving from a branch or, flying in one place, it descends vertically onto its prey.

43

The white-tailed deer is seen frequently along forest edges in British Columbia. Timid, it follows forest trails looking for thick grass.

a spruce tree. Eagles always prefer to perch at the mouth of a river in the hope of catching salmon that have been weakened by their long swim, making them easy prey. In summer several dozen raptors assemble along the Portland Canal. Five species of salmon inhabit the waters near Hyder; Salmon River and Fish Creek are among the most important upstream spawning grounds for chum salmon. Forested zones along the route attract porcupines and squirrels. The forest itself is a mixture of spruce and poplars, the understory a mixture of alder, salmon berry, and devil's club bushes. The tree line is 1,970 feet (600 meters) above sea level. Toward Salmon Glacier the countryside changes, becoming more arid. The trees grow farther apart, then disappear entirely, replaced by rock formations. This higher country is home to the marmots. By the end of the summer, they approach their maximum weight and frequently leave their burrows. Mountain goats also like to come out into this terrain of rock and ice, but sightings of them are much rarer.

44

The spirit of the black bear

Among the Gitksan—the "people of the river," as they call themselves—and the other tribes of British Columbia, the art of the totem reached its peak in the 1860s. These immense cedars, sculpted into real or mythical fetish animal images, invoke the spirits of the thunderbird, the cannibal bird, or sea monsters and recall the symbiosis that linked human and animal.

The black bear, so present in the life of the Indians, was represented often. A totem in the Gitksan style was placed on June 11, 1976, in Van Dusen Gardens in Vancouver. It tells the story of the black bear of the Orque clan: "A long time ago, a man went into the mountains to hunt goats. The black bear captured him and carried him off into its den. It did not kill him; on the contrary, it taught him many things, such as the art of catching salmon, in which men excelled from that time forward. After two years, the man was allowed to return to his people. But he had become so similar to a black bear that he frightened the people of his village. However, one of them recognized him and brought him home. He rubbed the man-bear with medicines until he regained his human form. The man, having once again become a man, thus took the black bear as a symbol and, when in difficulty, was sure to receive the aid of his friends the bears."

Totems in the Nisga's style make similar reference to the black bear. Here is the legend from one totem also at Vancouver: "A man went alone into the forest and asked the Spirit of the Forest: 'Why am I alone? Is there nobody here to help me?' The spirit answered: 'I will give you a black bear. If you can live in harmony with it, I will send you more of my children.' The man then learned to live in peace with the people of the forest. When he found himself alone on the sea, he called on the Spirit of the Sea, who gave him the killer whale. Noticing that the sky was empty, he called on the Spirit of the Sky, who sent him the crow.

"Man can live in peace with all the animals of the forest, of the sea, and of the air. If we can do this with so many different animals, we certainly can live in peace with all those among us."

PRACTICAL INFORMATION

When traveling in British Columbia, drivers must pay close attention to the road: bears may cross in front of a vehicle.

TRANSPORTATION

■ **BY AIR.** To Vancouver via Toronto on Canadian airlines, from Vancouver to Prince Rupert, Smithers, and Terrace, and even as far as Stewart coming from Ketchikan, Alaska.

■ **BY FERRY.** From Ketchikan or Prince Rupert, ferry service is available only from May to September, with five trips per month. Hyder features a small port with an open mooring, a boat ramp, and a seaplane.

■ **BY ROAD.** Hyder can be reached from Stewart in British Columbia by Route 37A. At the border crossing the road changes from asphalt (in Canada) to gravel (in Alaska). Cars may be left in a parking lot 2,000 feet (600 meters) from the site.

Drivers must use caution because the road leading to Fish Creek serves a mine, and trucks cross it frequently.

DISTANCES

From Vancouver to Terrace: 840 miles (1,355 km)
From Terrace to Stewart: 196 miles (316 km)
From Prince Rupert to Stewart: 287 miles (463 km)
From Whitehorse to Stewart: 661 miles (1,066 km)

LODGING

In summer the two campgrounds at Stewart fill quickly with large camping vehicles. Several motels, hotels, and restaurants exist between Stewart and Hyder.

CLIMATE

The area is influenced by marine climate. Summer is relatively hot, with pleasant evenings featuring temperatures 41–59 degrees F (5–15 degrees C).

PLACES TO VISIT

Between Terrace and Stewart, the Cassiar Highway, or Route 37, crosses many totem pole sites. Carved in giant cedars, the totems represent the cultural identity of the Gitksan and show their remarkable talents as observers of nature. The art of carving totems declined at the turn of the 19th century, but in the 1960s the Gitksan renewed their ties to their past and again began carving their giant images in wood. Traveling north from Terrace, Route 37 follows the shore of the Skeena River

K'san is a restored Gitksan village, an ideal place to discover the culture of Amerindians from British Columbia.

toward the village of Kitwanga. Once placed along the edge of the riverbank, the totems now stand farther back after a 1935 flood carried away the image of an eagle. A bit farther north is the village of Kitwancool, whose last totem pole was carved in 1994. Farther along Route 16 is the town of Hazelton, where the historic village of K'san has been restored. The village houses have painted facades, and there are carved totems showing figures representing various clans: the Wolf, the Frog, the Eagle, and the Bear. North of Hazelton, the village of Kispiox, along the river of the same name, has some very old totems. Some are stored in a shed to preserve them, but copies are being built. Notice that most of the bears shown on the totem poles are grizzlies.

A few miles from Stewart lies Bear Glacier, one of the few easily accessible blue glaciers in the world. Salmon Glacier, in contrast, 12.5 miles (20 km) from Hyder, is accessible only from July to October. The route leading to Salmon Glacier is rough and winding, but the view is worth the detour. Hyder features the oldest stone house in Alaska, constructed by D. D. Gaillard, and a museum that traces the history of the first gold prospectors in the region. Signs of former silver and gold mines remain visible along the trails. In summer the U.S. Forest Service maintains an information center at Hyder for the Misty Fjords region of the Tongass National Park.

RECOMMENDATIONS

If you encounter a bear on the road, stop or slow down, because it may be a female with young following. Along the road between Hyder and Fish Creek, if a bear comes down the slope, you must not stop because other vehicles will also stop, thus preventing the bear from returning to its fishing site, and perhaps provoking an aggressive response. Food with a strong smell must never be prepared in the parking lot near the observation site because it might attract a very excited grizzly.

45

Observation

Black bears can be seen at Hyder between July and September, when they take advantage of the return of the chum and pink salmon and complete their nourishment with the berries and plants found along the riverbank. They are very cautious as they fish, preferring to remain hidden in the high vegetation along the shore, and moving almost imperceptibly through the foliage. They watch the salmon in the water for several moments, then grab their prey with a single swipe of a paw. They also may be satisfied with a dead and decomposing salmon. They then leave the riverbank to enjoy their snack where they cannot be seen. They generally climb back up the slope leading to the forest, which is separated from the river by the road that connects Hyder and Salmon Glacier. The bears cross that road several times a day.

Upon arriving at the fishing spot, one frequently sees a bear on the slope in a forest clearing, eating berries with apparent great enjoyment. The bears appear near the river mainly early in the morning and late afternoon.

Black bears share this spot with grizzlies. They may exchange fishing locations, but they do not fish at a location at the same time. The grizzlies are much more demonstrative and may spend one or two hours in the riverbed pursuing salmon.

A female common merganser, also known as the great sawbill, takes her ducklings across a bear site without worrying whether a grizzly might be bathing nearby.

Canada (Manitoba): Riding Mountain National Park

Riding Mountain National Park is located 140 miles (225 km) northwest of Winnipeg in the province of Manitoba. It was established in 1933 on the site of a former forest reserve that had been set aside in 1895. In June 1986, the park was named a Biosphere Reserve. Its highest point, 2,480 feet (756 m) above sea level, is also the highest point of a 360-mile (580-km) ridge that is part of the Manitoba Slope, which begins at the shore of the glacial Lake Agassiz. The slope rises abruptly from 1,384 feet (422 m) above the prairies and separates the plains of Saskatchewan and Manitoba. The central plateau of North America is covered with thick glacial deposits consisting of sand, clay, and gravel, which are the origins of the various terrain features—moraines, straits, potholes, lake gorges—that are numerous within the park.

The region is one of transition between northern forests, the wooded zones of the east, and the prairies of the west. Riding Mounting National Park is a veritable island of greenery hidden amid immense fields of grain. Its rich and varied vegetation provides an ideal habitat for large forest animals. Thus, moose, white-tailed deer, elk, bears, and wolves share a territory of 1,131 square miles (2,976 square km) composed of northern forest, aspen forests, and grasslands.

Wild fires are a natural phenomenon here, one that helps preserve the balance of the system. They thin tracts of forests that have become too dense, promoting the establishment of new species and the diversification of the best adapted, thus allowing numerous species of birds and small mammals to feed and find shelter.

The park provides 32 hiking trails, covering 198 miles (320 km). They may be covered on foot, on mountain bikes, or on horseback.

47

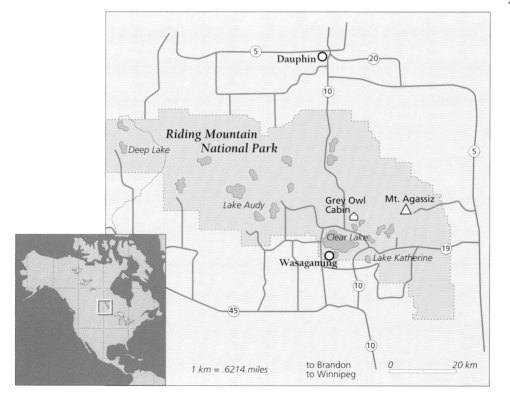

Flora and fauna

The park includes three major ecosystems: mixed forests of oak and aspen to the east, forests of spruce and aspen in the northern part, and prairies to the west.

Forests cover 78 percent of the park, and the tree species are varied. At the highest elevations are spruce, gray pine, balsam, false aspen, larch, and paper birch. At the foot of the slope, in the lowest and warmest area, open woods are interspersed with bushes, ferns, vines, and, in the western part of the park, vast prairies covered with wildflowers that begin to bloom in early summer. Among the 400 recorded species of plants, 17 are classified as rare in Manitoba.

Near Lake Audy, a population of 30 bison inhabits a partially wooded plain of 1,598 acres (647 hectares). They cross the plain in early morning to reach their water supply, then return in late evening. Among the large ungulates (hoofed mammals), one may see moose, white-tailed deer, and elk. According to 1995 population estimates, 5,000 elk and 6,000 moose live in the park. In autumn, during rutting season, the forest resounds with their calls. Besides the black bear, carnivores include the coyote, the red fox, the wolf, the lynx, and several mustelids (small carnivorous mammals such as weasels). A population of 40 wolves soon will be the subject of a research program aimed at understanding the causes of this species' decline. The beaver is present everywhere. The many dams that it builds change the terrain, and it is often necessary to intervene to avoid the flooding of hiking trails in the spring. More than 230 bird species have been identified, including the bald eagle and the osprey, both of which nest in the park. Most of the bird species are migrants that arrive in May. The region of Riding Mountain is known worldwide for its 69 species of butterfly. The lakes are full of fish: pike, yellow perch, and trout are abundant. Lake trout and rainbow trout inhabit Lake Katherine and Deep and Clear Lakes.

48

Early in the morning, the bison cross the plain to reach their watering hole. Massive and combative animals, they only fear the wolf and man.

Observation

The varied habitats within the park are favorable for the development of the black bear population. Studies of females have shown that their rate of reproduction is the highest in North America: females give birth to an average of three young, and as many as five may be born in a single delivery.

The population is 900 bears within the park and 500 to 600 more in the region surrounding it. No bear is completely free of danger: outside the park, hunting by Native Americans is allowed, and poaching goes on even inside the park. The same study showed that over a three-year period only a third of the bear population survived, and that of the two-thirds that died, 75 percent were killed by hunters.

In September the large male moose prepare for rutting season and lose the velvet on their antlers. Approached by canoe at five A.M., this specimen did not flee.

Grey Owl (1888–1938)

He was called the "ambassador of the animals." His personality marked his era, which was that of the "hunters of the woods" and of the discovery of the Canadian Great North.

Grey Owl, the Hibou gris, or Wa-Sha-Quon-Asin in the Indian language, was of an Apache mother and a Scottish father. The Ojibway Indians taught him all the secrets of the forest and the hunt. It was they who gave him his nickname, because he loved most of all to go out exploring after night fell. He loved the wildlife and lived for a long time with the beavers. He was so well accepted among them that, when he came to stay in Riding Mountain National Park in 1931, he made the trip with an entire family of beavers! He recounted anecdotes about them: "Together we made a trip of some thousands of miles, the beavers in a large rolling tank specially constructed for them, with me in the rear in a baggage wagon. It took us about a week to reach Riding Mountain, which was our destination. It was quite a stern test." At that time, the park already was surrounded by agricultural land: "I lived in the high oasis of Riding Mountain which, with its poplar forests and peaks covered with flowers, was like a huge island of green hanging over the dry and burning monotony of the wheat fields of Manitoba."

When the site proved unsuitable for beavers, he left for Prince Albert Park, where he established Beaver Lodge, a cabin adapted for the cohabitation of man and beavers. In his youth, when he was employed as a boatman or porter or forest warden in the summer, he left to discover the Canadian Great North. In winter he returned to his hunting grounds to trap fur-bearing animals. He wrote his life story at Beaver Lodge in the book *Ambassador of the Animals*, which made him known in all of North America.

During his expeditions in the Canadian forests, he encountered black bears on many occasions. Here is what he recalled of his impressions: "They all are good guys, inoffensive and well-groomed, who pay not the least attention to two-footed beasts; it is quite a frequent thing to come nose-to-nose with one of these citizens while peacefully walking along the highway."

49

Grey Owl shared his cabin with a family of beavers. Very plentiful before the arrival of the colonists, the beavers returned throughout Canada after intensive hunting ended.

50 The black bear eats almost exclusively acorns when they are abundant in autumn. It supplements its diet with wild apples and sometimes invades agricultural land and areas where bait has been set.

In early autumn, the first frosts color the leaves red and yellow. The end of September is the ideal time to traverse the Canadian forest.

Every year, 200 to 300 bears are cut down in this way.

Not all the bears of this region are black: in a sample of the bears captured in 1987, 1988, and 1989, 45 percent were grizzlies, 30 percent chocolate, only 22 percent completely black, and 3 percent cinnamon. Some bears are even bicolored, with the colors arranged in various patterns. The black bear uses different habitats in the park: poplar and coniferous forests and marshes in the daytime, and at night it moves into cultivated areas.

In autumn the bear moves around a great deal to feed and build up its fat reserve: a twenty-four-year-old female is known to have traveled up to 186 miles (300 km) within a few days. The bears consume a varied diet. Oak forests provide a large quantity of acorns. The bear establishes itself in a tree and pulls on branches full of acorns. It does not reject plums and apples and occasionally will venture into gardens.

Sometimes the bear will attack a young elk or moose in early spring, and it has been known to hunt beavers. Bears are also attracted by bait set by hunters and unfortunately become accustomed to easy sources of nourishment and become dependent on them. This presents a dual danger: the bear forgets how to hunt for itself and is in danger of being killed.

This period of intense food searching is the easiest time in which to find a bear in its natural habitat.

PRACTICAL INFORMATION

Autumn is the best time to discover Manitoba
because of the enchanting colors of Indian summer.

TRANSPORTATION

■ BY AIR. Canadian Airlines serves Winnipeg via Toronto.
■ BY BUS OR CAR. From Winnipeg the park can be reached by bus or car via Route 16. At the junction of Route 10, turn north to reach Wasagaming, where the main entrance of the park is located. The road crosses the park and leads to Dauphin, which is located 8.2 miles (13 km) north of the park. Route 19, which can be reached from the east, cuts across a steeply sloped part of the park. Every vehicle crossing the park must have an admission ticket, which can be obtained at the entrance.

DISTANCES

From Wasagaming to Brandon: 60 miles (95 km)
From Wasagaming to Dauphin: 43 miles (70 km)
From Wasagaming to Winnipeg: 155 miles (250 km)

LODGING

Camping is the best way to discover the natural environment. Numerous campgrounds offer various conveniences: 6 are fully equipped and accessible by car, 18 are farther away and offer only a water supply and toilets. Several locations, on the shores of the large lakes and linked to the road system, have cooking sheds with woodstoves and toilets. For those who want to travel on foot or by mountain bike, there are rudimentary campgrounds farther toward the interior of the park. The center of Wasagaming offers visitors numerous hotels, motels, and chalets, plus a wide variety of restaurants, food stores, and souvenir shops.

CLIMATE

Between the short, humid summers and the long, cold winters, the autumn offers pretty days, with morning frost and beautiful late-afternoon light. The precipitation is moderate: 6 inches (15 cm) of rain and 5 feet (150 cm) of snow is the yearly average; the average temperature ranges from 28 degrees F (–2 degrees C) in January to 61 degrees F (16 degrees C) in July.

PLACES TO VISIT

When passing through Winnipeg, plan to visit the Museum of Man and Nature to learn what life was like 450 million years ago, board a boat transporting pelts for the

The Museum of Man and Nature at Winnipeg is one of the most beautiful in Canada because of its very realistic replicas.

Hudsons Bay Company in the 17th century, and discover the paintings of the Cree Indians.

In the center of the city, whose name in Cree means "muddy waters," the Red and Assiniboine Rivers join at a place called the Fork. At one time, archaeological evidence shows that this was an assembly point for Native American tribes who followed the bison herds; researchers have found kitchen utensils, animal bones, and remains of houses. The Riel House is a home built in the 1800s; it belonged to the family of Louis Riel, who defended the territorial rights of the half-breed descendents of French

settlers and local people. These descendents were called "hunters of the wood" because they participated in the fur trade. In the park, a hiking trail leads to the cabin where the naturalist Grey Owl stayed, and from which he observed beaver populations. Objects found at that location, some as old as 4,000 years old, indicate that native populations used this region for fishing and hunting.

An educational program has been set up to help people discover the park. At Wasagaming the interpretation center contains exhibits of the park's animal specimens and gives slide shows. From May to September, experts are present to answer questions. In the summer, guided walks, activities for children, audiovisual presentations, and educational films are available. Night hikes are set up to observe fauna by flashlight. In the mating season, a stop in the park allows you to hear the herds of elk and white-tailed deer communicating. Researchers specializing in the study of the black bear, wolves, elk, moose, coyotes, beavers, and Arctic hares also lecture on the life patterns of these mammals.

51

Observation site

United States (Tennessee and North Carolina): Great Smoky Mountains National Park

With steeply rising mountains and luxuriant forests, crystal-clear water, streams, and a rich variety of fauna, the Great Smoky Mountains National Park is a paradise that the naturalist may never want to leave. The park was created in 1934 on a territory of 5,928 acres (2,400 hectares) of private and commercial land purchased with donated money. Subsequently, it has been named an International Biosphere Reserve.

The name Smoky comes from the cap of mist that, like wisps of smoke, envelops the mountains and descends into the valleys. The Cherokee people named it "the place of the blue smoke."

The park is located in the southern part of the Appalachian Mountain chain, between Tennessee and North Carolina. These mountains, which are among the oldest in the world, were formed by igneous and metamorphic rocks dating from the Precambrian era. They are crossed by the Appalachian Trail, which links Georgia and Maine and is 2,100 miles (3,400 km) long. Between three and four million visitors hike the trail each year, but only about a hundred of them cover the full distance. The trail crosses 68 miles (110 km) of the park, half of which is higher than 4,920 feet (1,500 m); the highest point on the trail is Clingmans Dome, at 6,642 feet (2,025 m). This section shows the entire trail's rich natural heritage.

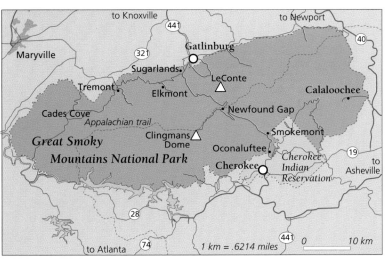

Flora and fauna

Since the last glacial period, the park has been a refuge for numerous species of animals and plants that have found ideal living conditions in the upper levels of the Smokies. Today some 1,500 species of flowering plants have been identified, of which 10 percent are rare. There are 4,000 species of nonflowering plants. Ninety-five percent of the park is forested, 25 percent of which is old forest, with trees reaching 20 feet (6 m) in circumference. This forest mass is one of the

The raccoon uses the many waterways of the park to wash its food.

most important temperate forests in North America. Coniferous forests of spruce and pine grow along the ridges, at altitudes of more than 5,900 feet (1,800 m). At lower elevations, the slopes are covered by deciduous trees: oak, poplar, American walnut, cherry—about fifty species in all. In June and July, rhododendrons, laurels, magnolias, and azaleas all burst into bloom. This display lasts all summer and peaks in autumn. Nearly fifty species of mammals inhabit the park. White-tailed deer can be observed at Cataloochee. The fawns that are born in spring are camouflaged in the dense vegetation. They move cautiously, fleeing at the slightest alarm. The black bear is considered one of their predators, but the bears attack only sick or wounded fawns. In moist areas, the bear shares its territory with

raccoons, squirrels, opossums, and river otters. The raccoon feeds a great deal in autumn, eating everything it finds and soaking its food in water to ease digestion. It finds refuge in hollow trees or holes in the ground, the same habitat as that of the black bear.

Some 200 species of birds have been identified, 38 species of reptile, 58 of fish, and 40 of amphibian, of which 27 are salamanders. The salamander population is the most diverse in the world. Among the salamander species native to the park are the Saint-Jacques de Rugel grass salamander and the Appalachian woodland salamander. New species are discovered each year.

Observation

The park is one of several places in the eastern United States where black bears still live in their natural habitat. All the bears in the park are black. The population is between 400 and 600. They remain far from sectors inhabited by humans, preferring to stay on the heights, in wooded areas, or in areas with dense brush. Population density is about one bear per square kilometer. One distinctive characteristic of the bears in the park is that they spend the winter in hollow tree trunks, not on the ground but above it, for better protection against the cold and dampness. They leave their hiding place if disturbed or if the weather turns warm.

Since 1991 a park team has been responsible for tranquilizing and removing "problem" bears that approach visitors too often. This procedure is harmless, but the bear now associates humans with disturbance and avoids inhabited areas. Some introduced species, such as the wild boar, compete with the bears for acorns and other foods. A new threat to the habitat is the progressive destruction of the oaks by a new parasite. The bears risk not only losing an important sousrce of nourishment, but also their hibernation areas. In 1972, for example, a year that produced few beechnuts, 252 human-bear incidents were recorded, most of them attributable to male bears. Forced to move farther to feed, many of them were killed by hunters. Some years are favorable for the bears in terms of food supply, and these are likely to see fewer human-bear

53

incidents. A park biologist noted in 1995 a bumper crop of acorns, beechnuts, walnuts, and other nuts (the best production ever recorded), on which bears feed in the autumn. However, other problems plague the bears: automobile traffic is involved in 71 percent of incidents; fences cut off their territory; and encounters with unleashed dogs are increasing.

The Cherokee

The history of Cherokee Indians in North Carolina extends back more than 1,000 years. Their society was based on hunting, trading among tribes, and agriculture. Social life was organized by a council of seven tribes.

When the Europeans arrived, the Cherokee adopted their tools and their firearms, both of which profoundly influenced their mode of life. They began to hunt not only for food but also for commerce. Forced to sign treaties, first with the English, then the Americans, they were progressively driven from the entire eastern United States. When gold was discovered in Georgia, Indian lands were confiscated, and the Cherokee were exiled farther west; families were forced to migrate to Oklahoma and Arkansas. Beginning in 1838, about 14,000 followed this route. More than 4,000 died of cold, hunger, and disease during the long six-month trek, which is still known as the "Trail of Tears." Then and earlier, the Cherokee suffered greatly from diseases brought by Europeans. Attempting to protect themselves, they devised the Dance of the Bear in winter: they moved clockwise around a fire, waddling and dragging their feet, their bodies and heads leaning from one side to the other in time to the drum. Accompanied by his clicking calabash, the leader growled like a bear. The others answered by growling in turn, raising their heads and swiping the air with their paws. They pretended to dance like the bears, which, in the forest, circled around a hemlock tree, leaving teeth marks on the bark at the same height as a man. Sometimes the leader also imitated the comic somersaults of the black bear. Here is the Cherokee "Legend of the Bear": In the tribe of Ani-Tsa-gu-hi, there was a boy who spent all his days in the mountains. As time went on, he spent even longer there. Finally he did not even return home to eat. His parents noticed that his skin was covered with long brown curls of hair. The boy explained to them, "There, in the woods, there is much to eat, and it is better than here. Soon I will be ready to return, and I will remain there." His parents were very worried, but their son reassured them: "Come with me, there is enough to eat for everyone. You no longer will have to work to feed yourselves. But if you come, you must fast for seven days." The parents sought the advice of the men of the tribe, who held a council and decided to follow the boy after they had fasted for seven days. When the other tribes heard news of this, they sent a messenger to convince them not to leave their village. But during the seven days, the men of the Ani-Tsa-gu-hi tribe changed greatly, and long brown curls of hair grew all over their

bodies. "From now on," they told the messenger, "you must call us Yonv(a) [bear]. When you are hungry, come to the forest and call to us with this chant." With those words, they left. When the messenger turned, he saw only a group of bears entering the forests. "Aho! We all are relatives!"

54

PRACTICAL INFORMATION

With part of it in Tennessee and part in North Carolina, the park is very accessible.
Every year 8 to 10 million visitors come.

TRANSPORTATION

■ BY ROAD. From Knoxville, Tennessee, take Route 441 to Sevierville, then follow the signs to Gatlinburg. The road follows the park until Cherokee. From Asheville, North Carolina, take Route 19 to Cherokee, crossing the Cherokee Indian Reservation.

DISTANCES

From Gatlinburg to Cherokee: 34 miles (55 km)
From Knoxville to Asheville: 112 miles (180 km)

GETTING AROUND

After parking their car, visitors sometimes find themselves out in the wild. The park is transected by 850 miles (1,370 km) of man-made trails of various types, from the most accessible to the steepest and most difficult. Travel by horseback is authorized on some of them. For camping in the backwoods, a free permit is required: it must be requested at the reservation office, and must show a day-by-day itinerary. Food must be brought in, and all trash removed. Reservations can be made one month in advance for a maximum of seven consecutive nights.

LODGING

There are ten campgrounds in the park, all equipped with water, campfire locations, tables, and toilets (there are no showers). Camping is limited to seven nights between May 15 and October 31, and to fourteen nights between November 1 and May 14. For groups, the recommended campgrounds are at Cades Cove, Elkmont, and Smokemont. In the backwoods, shelters can be used for only one night and camping

grounds for a maximum of three consecutive nights. The LeConte Lodge, which is accessible only by foot (a half-day's walk), provides lodging from mid-March to mid-November, with reservations required. Most of the towns in the vicinity have food, lodging, showers, and private camping.

CLIMATE

March is the most unpredictable month, with snowfall still possible. In mid-June, heat and humidity dominate, with frequent downpours in the afternoon. In mid-September the days are generally hot and sunny, the nights usually clear and cool, but rain and cold are not unusual.

PLACES TO VISIT

The visitor who arrives in Tennessee is greeted at the Sugarlands Center, which provides year-round information, publications, and films. In North Carolina, the Oconaluftee Visitors Center has a farm museum that shows the lifestyle of the first mountain pioneers with outbuildings for smoking fish and storing apples, a barn, and a corncrib.

In the town of Cherokee at the foot of the Great Smoky Mountains, a museum traces the life of the Cherokee Indians, who formerly populated a vast area. Those who escaped enforced relocation in 1838 took refuge in the Great Smoky Mountains, then returned to North Carolina, where they formed a tribal corporation in 1889. Today their population numbers 7,500. On September 21 at Oconaluftee, the Mountain Festival of Life is held. One- and two-day academic programs are organized by the University of

Tennessee in collaboration with the scientific staff of the national park.

These two locations are connected by the Newfound Gap Road, which crosses the Smokies. East of the park is the Cades Cove Center, a collection of old buildings dating from the end of the nineteenth century: mills, barns, churches, log cabins, and outbuildings. It is open from mid-April through October.

The Natural History Association of the Great Smoky Mountains offers training courses at Tremont. In addition, about fifty programs study the fauna, flora, and history of the park.

RECOMMENDATIONS

Find out about the special rules that must be observed in the park. Failure to obey them may result in a $500 fine and/or six months in jail.

Be alert for snakes and other hazards. Two species of poisonous snakes are found in the park. Every year one or two cases of snakebite occur. Poison ivy is common.

Don't bring pets. Domestic animals are forbidden on the park trails.

Dispose of waste carefully. There are special, bear-proof trash containers. Smokey the Bear, the symbol and animated spokesperson of the park (with his famous Ranger's hat) has for many years requested that visitors protect all of America's national parks.

55

Grizzly (Brown) Bear

Bear

(Ursus arctos)

Description

Average length: Adult, 66–109 inches (170–280 cm). **Shoulder height:** 35–58 1/2 inches (90–150 cm). **Average weight:** For males average weight varies according to the region from 297–858 pounds (135–390 kg). Females' weight varies from 209–451 pounds (95–205 kg). The largest individuals weigh 1,496 pounds (680 kg); newborns 105–175 ounces (300–500 gr); they weigh about 8.8 pounds (4 kg) when they first leave the den.

The adult grizzly bear is a massive animal with wide shoulders. The sexes show a noticeable difference in size, but not in other respects. Seen in profile, the head is concave, with a strongly marked forehead and muzzle. North American brown bears have a hump between the shoulders. The forepaws have very long claws, averaging 3.5 inches (9 cm), and reaching 4.7 inches (12 cm), that are used to dig roots from the soil or to unearth anthills. The grizzly is polymorphic, with important variations in color and size. Coloration may vary from dull brown, nearly black, to yellowish white, with all the variations of brown and red between those extremes. The name grizzly comes from its characteristic fur color, a mixture of brown and dull gray or yellowish that gives it a grizzled look.

Habitat

Habitat varies, ranging from tundra in northern Alaska to dense forest, passing through subalpine grasslands and plains. The grizzly bear is usually solitary, with males occupying very large areas (as much as 950 square miles [2,500 square km] in Yellowstone Park) that partially overlap the areas occupied by females. Within the area, the bear establishes a center of activity where it has regular access to food and sexual partners. It visits sites on a seasonal basis, depending on the presence of food.

Movement

The amount of territory that adults occupy depends on the region's resources. In northern Alaska, an area with a scant food supply, an adult male may cover 912 square miles (2,400 square km). Farther south, in areas rich in salmon, a bear needs only approximately 10 square miles (27 square km). Females occupy an area about six times smaller than that of males.

Food

This species is omnivorous, although its diet consists mainly of plants. What is consumes may include up to

Double page preceding. A grizzly does damage in a salmon spawning ground.

58

In the great expanses of North America, the grizzly bears find a varied diet, from large ungulates to small burrowing mammals, plants, and various types of salmon.

80 percent berries, roots, leaves, and grasses, with proportions of plant types varying by season and region. The remaining percentage of the diet includes insects (ants, butterflies), fish (salmon), mammals (from mice to deer), and carrion. The grizzly bear adapts its consumption to the local resources that it can obtain in the largest quantity with the least effort. If it eats materials unsuitable for its digestive system that are not well absorbed, it must ingest large amounts to obtain the necessary amount of nourishment. In good weather, it can thus spend time grazing on grasses and harvesting berries. Each day it can consume as much as 88 pounds (40 kg) of food and gain as much as 4.4 pounds (2 kg).

60

Predators

Only the young are prey to a few carnivores, such as the wolf, the puma, or the lynx.

Longevity

In the wild, the grizzly bear may live up to thirty years.

Maturity

Females reach maturity about the age of four; males reach sexual maturity at age five, but are not large enough to mate until they are eight to ten years of age.

Range

The grizzly bear is found on three continents in the entire temperate zone from 30 degrees to 70 degrees north latitude. It is the most widely distributed bear in the world.

Today the bear in the United States lives in Montana, Idaho, Washington, Wyoming, and Alaska. Farther north it inhabits western Canada. In Europe it has been confined to areas unsuitable for agriculture. Now it exists in Eastern Europe (Romania, Slovenia, Bulgaria, and the Czech Republic) and in some isolated mountain ranges of Western Europe (the Abruzzi, the Cantabrian Mountains, and the Pyrenees) and Scandinavia (Sweden and Norway). The grizzly bear is still well represented in the Commonwealth of Independent States, especially in Kamchatka and eastern Siberia.

A grizzly climbs the slope of an extinct volcano (Kamchatka).

Population

In 1995 the estimated population was 225,000 individuals. Since then, that figure has declined.

History

Humans and grizzly bears have lived side by side for a long time. In prehistoric times, they shared the forest. But although primitive hunting techniques and the beliefs of ancient peoples permitted them to coexist for millennia, agricultural civilizations have profoundly changed their relationship. Farms have expanded at the expense of forest, and people began raising livestock, both of which have put humans and bears in conflict.

Imprisoned as a circus animal in ancient times, the animal appeared later in menageries, zoos, and the cages of animal trainers. In the Middle Ages, bears became the prey of royalty, and hunting them became a sport. Noblemen hunted the bear with daggers, spears, and pitchforks. Because of these activities, the grizzly bear disappeared from the British Isles around the fifteenth century and vanished later from northern Africa and Syria. In the United States, the grizzly was eliminated from 98 percent of its range of 48 states after the arrival of the Europeans. In Europe it was gradually pushed into the mountains and deep forests. Although it was hunted down, the bear still struck fear in humans, and in many places its name

was never spoken. The Finns named it "apple of the forest," "strapping lightfoot," and "bluetail." The Lapps called it "the old man with a fur coat." Its name in Russian means "honey eater" (*medved*), while for the Yukaghir people of Kolyma in Siberia, it is "the big man" or "he who possesses the earth."

Now protected in many countries, the bear still is the victim of poachers who seek its bile or other by-products used in Asian medicine. Some stockbreeders still see it as a dangerous predator. It is also killed by hunters looking for trophies or thrills, hunted using traps baited with carrion, set upon by dogs, or massacred in its den as it hibernates. Finally, every day logging infringes on its remaining territory, shrinking

61

A female and her two young leave the forest to prowl along the shore.

its habitat even more.

The grizzly bear has nevertheless promoted the exploration of Kamchatka and the far eastern part of Siberia as many adventurers used the pathways that it forged in the wilderness. In those regions the bears are reputedly not aggressive toward people, which has enhanced their chances for survival.

In Yellowstone National Park in the United States, the grizzly bear has become a gauge of the biological health of the park.

Life cycle

All grizzly bears spend the winter, when their food is in short supply, in a den. The den may be a cave, a space between rocks, an open-air resting place, or, the most frequent location, a burrow dug by the animal within the roots of a spruce or a birch. These burrows are shaped like flattened ovals. The floor is covered with pine branches, myrtle twigs, or any other available plant material.

In autumn the pregnant female establishes herself in a cave or among tree roots. As with other bear species, the grizzly's winter sleep is more a state of inactivity than actual hibernation.

It is not rare in Eastern Europe, for example, to find traces of a bear in the snow during a midwinter warm spell.

In January or February, the female gives birth to two, perhaps three young; occasionally four may be born. Blind and lacking fur and teeth, the cubs are only able to find the six teats of their mother, who remains asleep. The milk contains 20 percent fat and allows the young to grow rapidly during their first weeks.

Their time in the den varies from one to seven months, depending on climatic conditions and the age and sex of the individuals. Generally the cubs' first departure is in April or May. For one year the cubs remain with their mother, who forces them away at the beginning of their second spring when she is ready to mate again. The first year is the most difficult for the cubs, and 40 percent of them do not survive that period.

Wolves, lynx, and pumas may attack cubs who have become separated from their mother. Aggression by a male bear is not uncommon because the departure of the female from the den with her cubs coincides with the mating season (from the end of May to the beginning of July).

On a hot August afternoon, a grizzly goes for a bath.

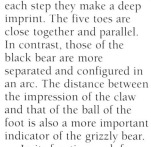

The estrus period of the females lasts for only about fifteen days. After that the bears usually return to the river mouths where salmon are swimming upstream. The abundance of this easy prey, rich in fat, allows the bears to rapidly build up a reserve of fat.

In areas where food is abundant, these normally solitary animals become gregarious. Females with their cubs must carefully avoid large males, who are always ready to attack a cub.

Indications of presence

In places where the black bear and the grizzly bear share territory, it is possible to differentiate between the two species by their footprints. The grizzly bear's rear claws measure 1.95–2.73 inches (5–7 cm). These claws are powerful and nonretractable, and with

Because of the long, powerful claws of its forefeet, the grizzly bear can scratch the soil to pull out the roots that it eats.

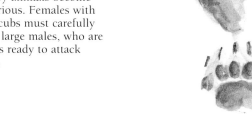

each step they make a deep imprint. The five toes are close together and parallel. In contrast, those of the black bear are more separated and configured in an arc. The distance between the impression of the claw and that of the ball of the foot is also a more important indicator of the grizzly bear.

In its frantic search for food, the grizzly bear leaves many signs of its presence. Because its digestion of the materials it eats is not especially efficient, the feces it leaves indicate precisely what its recent diet has been: berries, fish bones, mammal hair, plant material, and the like.

The grizzly bear uproots anthills, digging deep into them and leaving behind gaping holes that testify to its passage. In searching for roots or burrowing rodents, the bear scratches the soil vigorously, the marks of its claws remaining visible.

In most populated areas frequented, the repeated passage of generations of bears flattens the vegetation, creating pathways. During the salmon fishing season, the bear leaves behind many eviscerated fish and sometimes deposits fish in thickets. During the rutting season, sexually aroused large males attack trees, leaving deep claw marks on the trunks or breaking down shrubs.

63

Italy (Umbria): Abruzzi National Park

Established in 1923 to preserve the flora, fauna, and geological formations of the region, the Abruzzi National Park now is a refuge for numerous species that earlier lived all over the Apennines, such as the Marsican bear, the Apennine wolf, and the Abruzzi chamois. The first visitors' center in an Italian national park was established at Pescasseroli in 1969. In 1972 a center for ecological research in the Apennines was established, as was a 9,880-acre (4,000 hectare) natural wildlife reserve, the Camosciara. Between 1974 and 1993, study groups were founded for the wolf, the chamois, the bear, and the lynx. Today the park has an area of 98,800 acres (40,000 hectares) and is surrounded by a buffer zone of 148,200 acres (60,000 hectares). In the north, the park occupies the southern part of Marsica; its southern border is marked by

Mounts Meta and Mainarde, which are both about 6,560 feet (2,000 m) high. A good part of the park's eastern border coincides with the road connecting Alfedena and Scanno, which runs along the artificial Barrea Lake.

The park management is divided into four regions, which facilitates its management. The area around Camosciara, a mountainous region cut by the Fondillo and Lannaghera valleys and mostly covered by thick forests, is devoted to scientific study. The preservation area, which includes most of the park, is surrounded by a buffer zone where

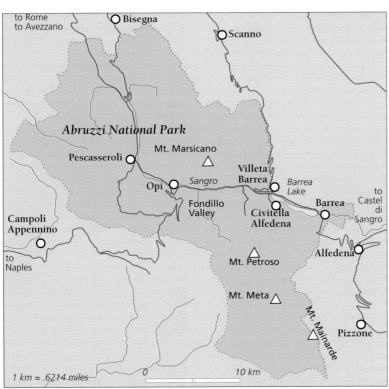

1 km = .6214 miles   0   10 km

traditional activities are allowed. Finally, the welcome center is included in an area accessible to tourists. Mountains are the dominant geographic feature of the park. The highest summit is at Mount Petroso, at a height of 7,370 feet (2,247 m). Vast forests extend into the high valleys, whose elevation is never less than 3,280 feet (1,000 m). The park is crossed by the Sangro River, which has its source in the northern part of the park and empties into Barrea Lake and contains a rich variety of fauna. A network of rivers and waterways flows through the Pescasseroli Basin. Glacier erosion has left its imprint on the terrain in the form of caves and grottoes.

Flora and fauna

Among the 60 species of mammals in the region, the Marsican brown bear, the Apennine wolf, and the Abruzzi chamois occupy a special place. For each, the park has created a system for surveillance, public

The forest in the Pescasseroli region.

A trough valley near Mount Marsicano.

awareness, and discussion. The populations are estimated at 70 to 100 bears, 40 to 50 wolves, and 500 to 600 chamois. Among the other mammals, the most important are the southern squirrel, the red fox, the wildcat, the marten, the weasel, the skunk, and the badger. The otter, formerly abundant, now is found only along little-traveled waterways. Populations of the red deer (500–600) and the roe deer (300–400) are the descendants of animals reintroduced into the park.

Among the 230 species of birds, golden eagles, of which not more than ten remain, have received special protection. The peregrine falcon, goshawk, eagle owl, tawny owl, barn owl, and scops owl are the region's other principal raptors. The old-growth forest provides habitat for the Lilford or Dalmatian woodpecker, which is very rare, the wood pigeon, the wall creeper, the alpine chough, the chough, the black redstart, and the rock partridge. The wet areas are frequented by the mallard, the purple heron, and little- and great-chested grebes. Among the 40 species of reptile present, the Orsini Viper is under protection. Forest covers 51,870 acres (21,000 hectares), or 70 percent of the protected territory. About 1,870 species of complex plants, grouped in three zones, have been identified. The first zone

The bear as a symbol

In Abruzzi Park, the policy of protecting habitat to provide bears with undisturbed areas has borne fruit and made the bear the park's symbol. Through negotiation, the boundaries of the park have been extended constantly to give the bears more living space. In 1969 98,800 acres (40,000 hectares) were added following agreements with local residents. The result was the classification of 9,880 acres (4,000 hectares) where no economic activity is permitted. Since that time, millions of tourists have been attracted by the bears. Today, the territory of the bear population is once again being restricted, and ongoing negotiations may result in 49,400 more acres (20,000 hectares) being added to the park and the creation of protected satellite zones outside the park. The overall result would be 1,235,000 acres (500,000 hectares), the largest protected area in Europe, located only 124 miles (200 km) from Rome. While the protection of the bears in Abruzzi can serve as an example for other places, we must not forget that the disappearance of the rural way of life and the financial gains generated from tourism favor such decisions. Conversely, experiments in species reintroduction conducted in another part of Italy, Trentino, ended in failure. The bears that were chosen had had too much contact with humans, and they caused numerous incidents. They were recaptured or killed. We must hope that the reintroduction attempted in the French Pyrenees will not end in failure, but will open the way for wider protection in the last wild mountains of France.

The bear fountain at Pescasseroli.

66

begins at the lowest level and extends to an elevation of 2,624–3,280 feet (800–1,000 m); the second rises to 6,232 feet (1,900 m), and the third comprises the summits, ridge lines, and high-altitude plains. In the high pastures, purple grass forms a dense carpet of vegetation. The old forest is dominated by beeches. Young shrubs grow next to crumbling trees 500 years old—thick giants with high, straight trunks that occupy the largest part of the Apennines. Other species live with the beech: the white maple, ash, mountain ash, and the Villetta Barrea black pine. At the lower altitudes, the riverbanks are lined with hornbeam, tufted oak, miniature and field maples, ash, poplar, and elms.

Some of the flowers peculiar to the park explode into bloom in the springtime: the park or Marsica iris, the lady's slipper, the epigogium (an orchid that grows only in Camosciara), the Alp anemone, the martagon and red lilies, the black orchid, and the columbine. To commemorate the symbiosis between nature and humans, each village has chosen a flower as its emblem. The village of Goia dei Marsi is represented by the "bear's ear" primrose.

PRACTICAL INFORMATION

About two million visitors come to the park every year.

TRANSPORTATION

■ **BY CAR.** It is easy to reach Pescasseroli, which is equidistant from Naples and Rome. From Rome, take the Rome-Avezzano-Pescara highway (A24/A25) to the Celano exit; then follow Route 83 toward Pescina, then Pescasseroli. From Naples, follow the Naples-Rome highway (A2) to Caianello; then take Route 85 toward Venafro, Rionero Sannitico, and Alfedena.

■ **BY TRAIN.** If you take the Rome-Pescara line, get off at Avezzano and continue on the ARPA line to Pescasseroli. If you take the Naples-Pescara line, get off at Alfedena and continue by train to Pescasseroli.

■ **BY BUS.** There is daily service to Avezzano and Castel di Sangro. In summer there is daily service from Rome to Pescasseroli.

DISTANCES

From Pescasseroli to Rome: 100 miles (160 km)
From Pescasseroli to Pescara: 89 miles (142 km)
From Pescasseroli to Naples: 103 miles (165 km)
From Pescasseroli to Venice: 366 miles (585 km)

LODGING

You may make a reservation in 1 of the 18 nearby villages. Pescasseroli is fully equipped with visitor's accommodations and has more than 500 beds in hotels of all types. Alfedena, Barrea, Villetta, Civitella, and Opi also have hotels, small pensions, inns, and lodgings in private homes. In the park, 20 campgrounds are near the villages, and other campgrounds have been developed in more remote areas.

CLIMATE

The region has very distinct seasons. Winter is very snowy, spring is full of flowers, and summer is sunny and temperate. Autumn brings rich colors, but the temperature drops considerably. The average temperatures: in spring, 45 degrees F (7 degrees C); in summer, 63 degrees F (17 degrees C); in autumn, 43 degrees F (6 degrees C); and in winter, 37 degrees F (3 degrees C).

PLACES TO VISIT

Five information centers serve visitors. At Pescasseroli, the park management's main office houses an information center, a natural history museum, an animal park, and a botanical garden. Villavallelonga offers a visitors' center and the Deer Museum. Near the visitors' center at Bisegna is the Abruzzi Chamois Museum and, not far along a marked route, there is a small park populated by several species of wild ungulates. Civitella Alfedena has another visitors' center, together with the Via Santa Lucia and the Apennine Wolf Museum. The Roe Deer Museum and the park museum are located at Campolio Apennino.

Also worth seeing is the exhibit Pizzone offers of the park's various habitats. During tourist season, guided hikes on horseback are organized. The Barrea Gorge is an area of the reserve rich in fauna and flora. Sixteen miles (25 km) from Pescasseroli are two protected areas for Atessa roe deer located in the Fucino, Gioia Vecchio, and Devil's Refuge Park.

RECOMMENDATIONS

Find out about hiking areas before planning your route. The park contains 150 marked naturalist trails. Entry is gained through twenty-five marked access points. Leaving the trails is forbidden.

67

Observation

In 1921, G. Altobello described a new subspecies of bear, the Marsican bear (*Ursus arctos marsicanus*), living in the Abruzzi. According to Altobello, the bear was endowed with special bony structures in the cranium and the palate. The Abruzzi bear, which has always been known by that name, today is not considered a true subspecies. The local people call it *urs*, or *urz*. The bear moves through closed valleys along the passes that separate them and frequents clearings.

A bear was killed in 1952 although hunting grizzly bears had been forbidden since 1939. In 1952 the grizzly bear population was between 150 and 180 individuals; today it is estimated at 70 to 100. In 1988 the Italian Ministry of the Environment forbade all hunting in certain areas contiguous to the park in order to protect the bear and limit poaching. Occasionally, a dead or abandoned cub is found; the females seem to have difficulty raising two cubs at the same time. The best times to observe the bear are between May 15 and June 15 and between September 15 and October 15. During those periods, the bear has a particular feeding pattern that makes it easy to locate. In spring observers must wait near the carcass of one of the numerous animals that did not survive the previous winter; eventually, a bear is likely to approach to feed on the carcass. The bear also feeds on wild spinach. At the end of the summer (August), it gorges itself on raspberries, wood strawberries, or gooseberries. In September and October, it prefers the wild apples that grow at elevations up to 4,000 feet (1,300 m). The inhabitants of the region have planted apple trees to keep the bears at a higher altitude, where they cannot attack their sheep. A program for the planting of corn was established in the region of Villavallelonga, 3,080–3,700 feet (1,000–1,200 m) above sea level, for the same reason. Before winter, beechnuts are an essential nutritional supplement, especially for pregnant females. Therefore, at that time of year, you have the best chance of seeing bears near beech trees.

A herd of Abruzzi chamois take advantage of the park's slopes.

Bulgaria: In the heart of the Balkans

Bulgaria occupies about one-fifth of the Balkan Peninsula. The country is bisected from east to west by an imposing mountain chain, the Stara Planina (old mountain) with eroded summits, whose highest peak is 7,318 feet (2,376 m). This mountain range is paralleled by another, the Sredna Gora (middle mountain) range. South of the latter range, the great Sofia Plain extends to the sea. At the bottom of the small valleys, in deep forests, the monasteries that once were a refuge for the hajduks remain as witnesses of the past. The southern part of the country is occupied by two other mountain formations, the Pirins and the Rilas, which include the highest peak in Bulgaria, Muss-Alla, 8,009 feet (2,925 m) high. Farther east, the Rhodopes Mountains are covered with beech forests, which give way at higher altitudes to firs and pines, then to pastureland through which rivers wind. The forests seem untamed because there has been only moderate exploitation of timber there.

Flora and fauna

Bulgaria, with its diverse climatic, geological, and topographic conditions, is home to 94 species of mammals, 383 species of birds, and 52 species of reptiles and amphibians. Among the animal species unique to Bulgaria are four species of reptiles, twelve of fish, and at least four of mammals. Five percent of the flora are unique to Bulgaria. Seventy-eight species of birds and ten of large mammals are classified as rare.

Early in the morning, in the dense mountains of Bulgaria, on the slopes and in sometimes-difficult terrain, it is possible to observe the great European fauna that find refuge from urbanization. In the Rila and Stara Planina Mountains, one may encounter

69

chamois; tufted, roe, and fallow deer; wild
boar; wolves; wildcats; red foxes; and
numerous birds of prey (golden, lesser
spotted, booted, and imperial eagles, griffon
and Egyptian vultures, goshawks, and
peregrine falcons). Mount Muss-Alla is
habitat for black grouse and wild goats, and
wild sheep are found in the eastern
Rhodopes. Crows and songbirds often
accompany hikers. Many of the 175 lakes in
the Pirin Mountains are full of fish.

The bear has long been a presence in the
area. Bulgarian tales are full of bears. A
Balkan proverb advises taking a doctor along
when hunting bears and taking a priest when
hunting wild boar. Legally considered a
nuisance animal, the bear was hunted until a
1941 law made it a protected animal. The
economic development of the country

Along the streams of Toja, many flowers grow
in rock crevices.

The Rhodopes Mountains offer a broad
perspective of the Bulgarian forests.

70

accelerated its decline, but since coming under protection, the species' population has again been growing.

In Bulgarian forests, which occupy 35 percent of the country, the tree species blend harmoniously: oaks, beech, elms, birch, and alpine and subalpine conifers. Most of the forests are natural. Some rare species such as silver pine and filberts brighten the Pirin area, which is a typical example of a mixed mountain system in a complex region. The Bulgarians harvest plants and herbs to concoct teas and syrups according to traditional peasant recipes. Rare plants are also used in modern pharmacology. In lowland Bulgaria, depending upon the amount of human disturbance, interesting mammals such as red and roe deer, polecat, badger, and pine and stone martens can be found. Woodland birds such as jay, turtle dove, short-toed tree creeper, and golden oriole are common.

Observation

Since 1941 the grizzly bear has been protected throughout Bulgaria. The best times of year to observe it are March and April and November and December. In April the fertile females remain near their dens for a time, which they prefer located on the north side of the mountains.

In the Stara Planina alone, the bear population is estimated at 800. In the mountains a bear uses an average territory of 7,410 acres (3,000 hectares), but the density varies according to the season. In the most favorable habitats, four or five individuals may share 2,470 acres (1,000 hectares), while in other situations a single bear may occupy 12,350 acres (5,000 hectares). Males are somewhat more numerous than females (53 percent and 47 percent, respectively, of the population). The population is rather young; only 10 percent are ten years of age or older. The diet consists of 75 percent plants and 25 percent wild and domestic animals. In spring meat is the predominant

71

Bear trainers

Symbolizing as it does what is wild in humans, and reminding us of our primitive origins, the bear has always fascinated us. Some mountain people, the famous bear trainers, have been able to take advantage of these long-standing emotions. In India and in the Carpathian and Pyrenees mountains, they have used the skill and intelligence of the bears to train them to perform stunts and acts at fairs and markets. A ring placed in the muzzle, through the sinus, gave them a sure hold on the "wild animal"; the incisors were sawed off and the claws filed. Thus, the master could simulate combat, in which he would always be victorious, without risk. Seeing the wild animal reassured villages that humans could master nature.

As in the Pyrenees, peasants practiced bear training in Bulgaria and Romania in times of financial crisis; the trained bears provided a significant supplementary income for their owners.

Bear trainers were abundant in the forests of the Balkan Peninsula, and most of those exhibited by the Gypsies came from the Carpathians and Transylvania. Unlike some Ariègois and Gypsies who crossed the Atlantic, the Romanians and the Bulgarians did not travel far. Their exhibitions brought them to neighboring countries, occasionally as far as France. They moved along their route in families, camping as they went. This practice, however, diminished significantly.

Unfortunately, with recent political changes and the ensuing economic crisis, this practice has reappeared. Bear trainers were forbidden in Greece and Turkey in 1995, and a center has been established in Greece to care for trained bears.

In Bulgaria it is difficult to see bears during the day. This rare picture of a Bulgarian bear shows its movement in the last snows of winter.

food, with sheep providing 67 percent, cattle 25 percent, and horses 6 percent. The bears are very active in this period. Most attacks occur in May and June and decrease in July. These feeding patterns explain why encounters with bears are frequent in spring, somewhat less so in summer, and rare in autumn and winter.

In January and February, the bear falls into a lethargic state and takes refuge in a den on a mountain slope or in a place in the forest from which it can see potential threats. Pregnant females usually choose a rocky cavity above the tree line. Tracks and signs of their presence are visible everywhere, especially on conifers that have been scratched along trails near the dens and sources of prey.

PRACTICAL INFORMATION

Gypsy villages still contain dozens of bears in captivity, which entertain tourists on the beaches of the Black Sea in summertime.

TRANSPORTATION
■ **BY AIR.** Several companies (Lufthansa, Air France, and Air Balkan) serve the city of Sofia.
■ **BY TRAIN.** If you fly to Paris, you can take a train to Sofia. There is a daily connection from Paris to Sofia via Budapest, a trip requiring 36 hours.
■ **BY CAR.** There are two possible routes: through Germany, Hungary, and Romania, or through Italy and Greece. To reach the Rhodopes, go to Plovdiv and drive toward Batchkovo. The Stara Planina extends north of Sofia to Sliven.

DISTANCES
From Sofia to Rila: 31 miles (50 km)
From Sofia to Plovdiv: 97 miles (156 km)
From Sofia to Karlovo (Valley of Roses): 91 miles (145 km)

LODGING
Visitors may stay in lodges and hotels or in double rooms in comfortable pensions. Lodging in forest cabins is more primitive. Typical local food is of good quality.

CLIMATE
In April and November the cold can be extreme, and snowfall is always a possibility. Between June and September, average temperatures vary between 66 degrees and 77 degrees F (19–25 degrees C).

PLACES TO VISIT
The Valley of Roses is a unique place of international renown. Because of its location—the valley, surrounded by the Stara Planina and the Sredna Gora, is watered abundantly by the mountain streams above—this is a favored spot where roses have been cultivated for more than three centuries. In May and June, carpets of white, pink, and red roses cover the valley. Kazanlak, the rose capital, includes a museum, and a garden growing 200 varieties of attar-producing roses and all the products of this cultivation (preserves, rose water, and rose liqueur).

The city of Sliven is surrounded by mountains, some of which, chalky and honeycombed with grottoes, resemble dolomite rock formations. They have been named the Sinite Kamani, or blue rocks, because they have a blue tint as twilight approaches.

Russia (Far Eastern Russia): Magadan region

Russia possesses territory with the densest brown bear population in the entire Northern Hemisphere, but only in a few areas can they be observed. One of the most accessible regions with a high bear population is the area around the city of Magadan, the capital of far eastern Siberia and better known as the transit center from which prisoners were sent to the Gulag camps (*Glavnoye upravleniye lagerey,* the central administration of the camps). With the population scattered across the entire region, the bears are quite easy to see along the Yama River (to the northeast) and in the Koni Peninsula.

The Koni site, east of Magadan, is formed by a continuation of the Kolyma mountain chain. Mountainous and wooded, it is crossed by numerous streams that hurtle down their steep slopes to join the Sea of Okhotsk to the south or the Gertner Bay to the north.

Very sparsely inhabited by humans, the Koni Peninsula and the nearby islands are the domain of brown bears that feed on upland grasses, berries, ants, and fish, depending on the season. Adjoining the very rich waters of the Sea of Okhotsk, the western part of the peninsula is classified as a reserve to protect its populations of bears and birds.

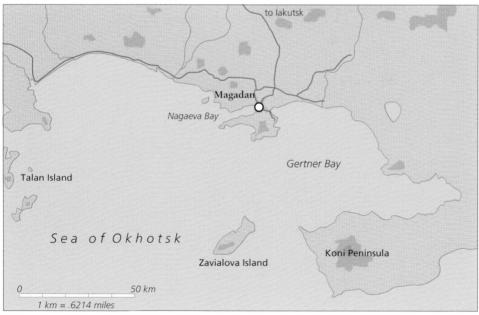

to Iakutsk

Magadan

Nagaeva Bay

Gertner Bay

Talan Island

Sea of Okhotsk

Koni Peninsula

Zavialova Island

0   50 km

1 km = .6214 miles

Flora and fauna

The rivers of the region are home to several species of the salmon family: the pink or Pacific salmon (*Oncorhynchus gorbuscha*), the chum salmon (*Oncorhynchus keta*), and the coho salmon (*Oncorhynchus kisutsch*). The scientific names are Russian, given to the species by the naturalist Georg Willem Steller at the beginning of the eighteenth century. In July the salmon begin their return to their spawning grounds, a process that changes the diet of the forest animals.

The estuaries are inhabited by Pacific gulls, black-headed gulls, and large-billed crows, which are always on the lookout for dead fish. Some distance from the shore, numerous mottled seals take full advantage of the abundance of fish.

The elk, those large ungulate inhabitants of the dense forests of the Northern Hemisphere, are common in this region. In the summer they come to lakes and rivers to drink and to protect themselves against mosquitoes.

In summer the grassy shores are covered with flowers such as the wild geranium, the Siberian iris, the fritillary flower, and other species.

74

On Talan Island, populated by seabirds, a ferocious red fox population has developed. They arrive on ice floes which connect the distance between the island and the continent.

The Evens

Before the large-scale arrival of Russians from the west, the region was inhabited by the Evens, who belong to the Evenk culture, undoubtedly one of the oldest in Siberia. Today, not more than 17,000 Evens remain. Hunters, gatherers, and fishermen, they formerly lived on the natural resources of the taiga: fur-bearing animals, salmon, berries, and plants and herbs whose uses they still remember. They also hunted the bear, whose name they never pronounced in winter for fear of awakening it, referring to it instead as "Cherne'si svir," "the wild black beast," treating it with respect and fear, and considering it a relative. A good Even housewife would never shake a bearskin outside the hut lest she cause a storm to arise. Indira Ardani, an ornithologist of Even ancestry, told us an intriguing story that she had heard from her mother: "A member of her family, known for his simple soul, became lost alone in the forest, on the other side of the river. Some days later, when his companions feared that he had been lost for good, he returned to the village. To the question that everyone asked him, 'How were you able to cross the river?' he answered simply, 'I got on the back of a swimming bear.' Nobody ever found out more about the subject."

An Even legend: How the sole came to be completely flat.

One day the sole fell asleep as it was warming itself in the sun at the very edge of the water. Just then the bear came out of the taiga. It was thirsty and wanted a drink. Seeing the sole, it flipped it up onto the shore with a swipe of its paw and said, "I am not hungry, but a sole is only a small mouthful. After my drink, I will eat it." Finding itself in a dangerous situation, the sole tried to bargain with the bear: "If you aren't hungry, you shouldn't eat. Come, let's have a little contest instead." "Is it any business of yours whether I eat or when?" growled the bear. "But tell me, what kind of contest do you want to have with me?" "What kind?" answered the sole, laughing. "It's very simple; we'll make a bet on who can last the longest, you under water or I out of water. If you win, you can eat me. And if I win, you will throw me back into the water." "All right," the bear agreed, and it jumped immediately into the water. It was hot, so why wouldn't it take a bath? It sank into the depths and remained there for a long time, until it had no more breath. Then it began to swim toward the shore to see what had happened to the sole, which was basking very calmly in the sun. It really was in great shape: a sole can survive in the air for a very long time. The bear, furious at losing, caught the sole and threw it back into the water. But as it picked up the fish, it flattened it so completely that today the sole is as flat as a pancake. It also became conical, whereas before it had been round. At least that is what any Even will tell you.

75

An old bear trap in eastern Siberia.

PRACTICAL INFORMATION

Because of the terrain to be covered and other difficulties, only group trips to observe bears can be made.

MAGADAN

The city of Magadan was built on Nagayev Bay, which opens onto the Sea of Okhotsk. It received its current name in 1932, when it expanded greatly because of the discovery of gold in the Kolyma Valley. Several million prisoners perished in the construction and expoitation of mines. Prisoners also left from Magadan for the Kolyma Gulags to the north. They had crossed the entire former USSR to Vladivostok, then arrived by boat in Magadan, which came to be called "the port of hell."

Now Magadan is a city of 150,000 that would like to forget its past. Nevertheless, a monument to the victims of communism was dedicated there in 1995. This large city, connected to Moscow by regular flights, itself offers little of interest. There is no tourism in Magadan and few artists except a few sculptors of mammoth tusks. The banks of the Kolyma River erode constantly, revealing fossils that testify to the richness of the Pleistocene fauna, including the bones of the woolly rhinoceros and of mammoths. Prospectors have only to bend down to collect them, then sell them at very high prices to professional carvers. From this primal material, polished and streaked with brown, some artists form especially fine items representing the animals of the region: brown bears, mountain goats, and snow leopards.

TRANSPORTATION

■ **BY AIR.** The Moscow/Magadan flight via Aeroflot takes between seven hours, thirty minutes and nine hours, depending on the flight plan. Flights depart from the Domededovo and Vnukovo airports. Since the opening of Russia, one can also reach Magadan from Anchorage, Alaska.

■ **BY CAR.** Magadan is connected with the rest of Russia by one road, which passes through Yakutsk. To reach areas of interest, helicopter is the easiest solution, but also the most expensive (1,500 dollars per hour in 1996). Boats also can be chartered.

DISTANCES

From Magadan to Yakutsk: 938 miles (1,500 km)
From Magadan to Talan: 60 miles (97 km)
From Talan to the Koni Peninsula: 97 miles (155 km)

LODGING

Magadan contains few hotels and only one restaurant worthy of the name, which also serves as a nightclub. At sites favorable for observing bears, tents can be pitched around fishing and hunting cabins after obtaining local authorization. From this point, you must be careful to obtain additional permission to explore the coast. Fishing is forbidden without an invitation from local residents, who know the idiosyncrasies of Russian bureaucracy.

CLIMATE

Because the area is on the Pacific, the temperature may reach 68 degrees F (20 degrees C) in the sun, but rain and fog can move in rapidly on the same day.

PLACES TO VISIT

In the large cities of Russia, the half-day wait between flight connections can be used to visit various points of interest.

In Moscow, the Zoological Museum offers the visitor impressive collections, although the displays are outdated. For the lover of Siberian fauna, one of the outstanding items is a complete skeleton of a Steller's rhytine, native to Sakhalin Island.

In St. Petersburg, the Zoological Museum founded by Peter the Great at the beginning of the eighteenth century displays some first-rate items, including some beautifully preserved specimens of polar and brown bear and an exhibit of Siberian mammoths. The Museum of Curiosities includes objects brought by travelers, beginning in the time of Peter the Great, such as shaman masks and totems. The anthropological collections abound with items originating with the Siberian and Aleutian peoples.

RECOMMENDATIONS

Educate yourself on potential hazards before departing. In July the mosquitoes are especially prevalent in the damp forests of Siberia. Provide yourself with mosquito netting and repellents, which cannot be obtained locally. The brown bears of Siberia are known to be docile. However, in August 1996 the photographer Mishio Hoshino was killed by a bear in Kamchatka. Great care is always recommended.

In forest clearings, the ermine, chipmunk, red fox, willow ptarmigan, and a variety of birds such as the willow tit, the redpoll, and the Kamchatka wagtail are quite easy for the patient observer to see. The nearby islands are frequented by numerous seabirds typical of the northwest Pacific: auks; white-necked, spectacled, and Brunnich's guillemots; puffins; pelagic cormorant; kittiwake; and Pacific gulls. The famous Steller's sea eagles, well known as fishing raptors, are especially attracted to this region by the auks and the nesting gulls. July is the month of flowers,

their cones begin to grow. The oily seeds of these conifers are an important part of the bears' diet in autumn.

Observation

The bears venture into the orchards a few miles from the towns, but beyond this it is difficult to specify a potentially successful observation site.

If you tell other visitors that you have come to see the bears, they will think you are crazy. There, people never go to observe bears, but to hunt them!

Male bears of far eastern Siberia reach an average weight of 660 pounds (300 kg). They are among the largest of the species, just after the grizzlies of Kodiak Island (Alaska).

The bears begin moving to their winter quarters at the end of October and remain sheltered until mid-May. It is in the summer, beginning in early July, that one should come to see them, when they are fully occupied in gathering dead salmon on the shore. If salmon are not available, the bears graze on grasses in forest clearings; in any case, the majority of their diet remains vegetarian. Unlike bears in other salmon-rich locations, the bears in this region have not developed a social existence.

Before flying out to sea, puffins congregate on the flat rocks at the entrances of their burrows and take a prolonged sunbath.

and the fields are covered with a mosaic of colors: the purple of geraniums and Siberian iris, the red of sedum, the pink of wild roses, the dark brown of the Kamchatka fritillary. The most common conifers, *Pinus siberica* and *Pinus pumila*, shift from green to rust as

Here, the bears are not considered dangerous, but it is still always wise to act with caution. Reports of accidents have always involved hunters who were carrying game with them, which attracted the bears.

If possible, do not carry food; and if camping, keep food stores far away from the camp site, preferably hanging from a tree out of the bear's reach since full grown grizzlies cannot climb trees.

77

Observation site

United States (Alaska): Denali National Park and Preserve

Mount McKinley National Park was established in 1917 as a wildlife reserve. In 1980 a decree on preservation of land in the national interest extended the park's borders to include 5.76 million acres (2.4 million hectares) and renamed the park Denali, which means "that which is high" in the language of the Athabascan natives. This national park, which already had been named an International Biosphere Reserve in 1974, has remained as the Athabascans knew it in earlier times. The park is divided into three zones: the full Denali reserve is the central, undeveloped region for which Mount McKinley National Park was created. Hiking there is tightly restricted, and hunting and sports are strictly forbidden. Along the borders in the second sector, designated

"national park," local residents are allowed to pursue activities to support themselves, using plants and fish. In the third zone, the Denali National Preserve, which is divided into two parts, tourists are permitted to hunt and fish, subject to the regulations of the Alaska Fish and Game Service.

The park is located at 63 degrees north latitude, at the center of a vast mountain range. The subarctic ecosystem attracts large mammals: moose, grizzlies, caribou, and wolves. Denali is known worldwide for its wild landscapes and the opportunities it

78

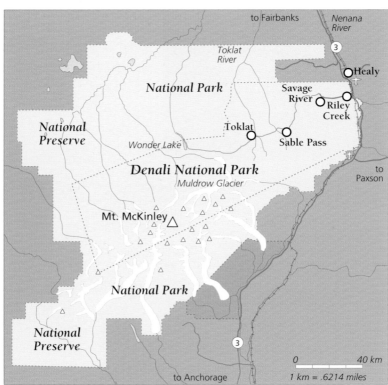

affords to observe animals. The delicate beauty of its tundra plants and the winding rivers at the bottom of large valleys give grandeur to the mountains, which are often covered with fog.

Mount McKinley is the highest peak in North America. With a base located at an altitude of 600 meters (1,968 feet), it has the largest vertical face in the world and has become a classic for mountain climbers. Its north peak was first conquered in 1910 by four gold prospectors who covered the 8,856-foot (2,700 m) slope in a single day. When they arrived at the summit, they discovered that the south peak is higher at 20,320 feet (6,197 m). In 1913 an expedition confirmed this observation. The head of the

The wolf is one of the other attractions of the Denali Park. It plays an important role as a large predator in controlling ungulate (deer and moose) populations.

79

Every day moose come to bathe in Wonder Lake, but Mount McKinley is not always so clearly visible.

expedition, Harry Karstens, was named administrator of the Mount McKinley park in 1917.

Flora and fauna

The park is home to a wide range of plant and animal species. In earlier times the Dall sheep was hunted, like caribou, for its meat. It avoids its principal predator, the wolf, by climbing the high mountain slopes where winter vegetation is eliminated by the wind. In the summer, the sheep feed on small alpine tundra plants. The park's population is about 2,500 individuals.

The Alaska moose, widely distributed in the park, is the largest of its species (a male may weigh as much as 1,496 pounds [680 kg]). In the interior of the park, gregarious caribou make large-scale migrations from the land where the females give birth in the spring to the summer pasturage. In autumn, the rutting period, the herd returns to its winter quarters in the tundra. Wolves avoid humans and are rarely seen. They live in packs consisting of a dominant male, a dominant female, and several other adults with a few young. They hunt together, feeding on moose, caribou, and sheep, attacking the weakest individuals. With the grizzlies, they play an important role as predators in the equilibrium of the park.

Among the small mammals in the park are beaver, Arctic hare, marmots, and several

The naturalists of Denali Park

In the early twentieth century, Charles Sheldon became the first naturalist to study the territory of the future Denali Park. He had a talent for observation and an acute sense of the natural environment. He took copious notes, which he edited into a book whose foreword was written by Harry Karstens, the park's first administrator. In the summer of 1906, Sheldon led a 45-day expedition into the Denali region to establish the distribution of the animal population. He wanted to repeat this experience over a longer period, so in 1907–08 he built a cabin near the Tokla River and spent the winter crossing the tundra with Karstens. The biologist Adolf Murie described him in these terms: "He studied the simplicity, the solitude, and the sensations of the elements and he sought a close relationship with the animals in the remote places of the mountains of Alaska."

It was he who proposed the name Denali for the lands that he wished to have protected, and it was because of his action that Mount McKinley National Park was established officially after nine years of discussion. The name Denali was adopted later. Two placards on the bridge over the Toklat River are dedicated to the memory of Sheldon and Karstens.

Their work guided the scientists who followed them: Olaus Murie, who in 1923 discovered the nest of a migratory sandpiper; his brother Adolph, who followed the beaver tracks along the shores of Wonder Lake in 1960, after having studied a pack of wolves from 1939 to 1941 to determine their role in the park and their eventual impact on the population of Dall sheep; Joseph Dixon; George Wright, who in 1926 identified for the first time a nest of a surfbird; Inez Mexia, Frances Payne, and many others.

species of squirrel that serve as appetizers for the bears and wolves. The wolverine and the lynx also feed on these small mammals.

Numerous migratory birds nest in Denali: the Arctic tern, the golden plover, the surfbird, and the long-tailed skua. Seventy pairs of golden eagles live between the Nenana River and Wonder Lake, the largest nesting population in Alaska. That group seems to be stable, and it is the subject of a research program in the park. However, at migration time the eagles are the victims of poisoning, electrocution, and illegal hunting, and they have also suffered a gradual loss of habitat. The transitional zone between tundra and taiga is inhabited by the short-eared owl, the willow grouse, the Lapland

bunting, and the northern harrier. In the spruce forests, the hawk-owl, the goshawk, and the sharp-tailed grouse find refuge. The gyrfalcon, the common gull, and the snow bunting are among the 159 species of birds that have been recorded at Denali.

The park's vegetation is typical of polar zones. The temperature and humidity vary greatly. The growing season lasts less than 100 days, with the permafrost (permanently frozen soil), restricting the drainage and the oxidation of the land. In the taiga or northern forest, white and black pine, balsam poplar, paper birch, and larches grow. Various species of berries grow at ground level.

At an altitude of 2,460 feet (750 m), damp tundra takes over, with dwarf birches

PRACTICAL INFORMATION

At an altitude of 20,313 feet (6,193 m), Mount McKinley is the highest peak in North America.

TRANSPORTATION

■ **BY CAR.** Denali is located 250 miles (400 km) north of Anchorage and 125 miles (200 km) south of Fairbanks. Access is via Route 3. You may drive your car 15 miles (23 km) into the park as far as the Savage River entrance, then you must transfer to a bus to enter the park. The only exception is a lottery held in September to authorize 400 cars to enter the park.

■ **BY TRAIN OR BUS.** Service from Anchorage and Fairbanks is provided daily in the summer.

■ **IN THE PARK.** Buses serve the visitors' center, the campgrounds, and the park offices. Various routes are suggested for viewing animals. Tour reservations must be made at least two days in advance, possibly more when the park is heavily visited between the end of May and mid-September. Some bus routes offer guided tours. The longest route takes 12 hours to complete, and visitors should bring food.

LODGING

One hotel is located in the park, and others are available in the vicinity. Seven campgrounds have been established within the park: three of them are open to private vehicles; the Morino campground is accessible only by foot. The other three are served by the park bus. The campgrounds charge a fee and places must be reserved two days in advance. Plan to camp outside the park when you arrive because the campgrounds are often full. Only the Riley Creek grounds are open year-round, but there is a 14-day limit on site use.

Finally, one can hike in the backwoods with an authorization at the visitors' center, authorization can be obtained only one day or less in advance. Two restaurants and a small store are located at the park entrance.

CLIMATE

Summers usually are cool, humid, and windy. Snowfall is possible. Bring clothing suitable for temperatures ranging from 32 degrees F to 66 degrees F (0–19 degrees C), as well as mosquito

repellent. The park roads may be closed because of bad weather.

PLACES TO VISIT

The visitors' center opens on May 26, with programs beginning on June 2. A list of the 90 research activities is available; these include studies of large mammals (wolf, caribou, moose, grizzly, and Dall sheep), dust measurement in the park, and a geological study. Rangers present 45-minute slide shows on a wide variety of subjects (the auditorium is located next to the park hotel). Beginning in June, short hikes are organized in various parts of the park. A short stroll takes you to a cabin that was used by rangers between 1922 and 1927, when the park was being established. Another walk of 30 to 45 minutes takes you to Mile 13, following the path that horsemen took to provide communication between the McKinley Station and the Muldrow Glacier. At Mile 42.9, at the bottom of the valley, is the Fork Ranger Cabin used by Adolph Murie when he was researching wolves in the 1940s.

81

and several types of willow. Above that, at 3,608 feet (1,100 m) comes dry alpine tundra, with saxifrage and potentilla, where blooms usually appear in mid-June.

Other lovely flowers in Denali include the blackish oxytrope and bell heather and higher on the ridges, woolly lousewort.

Observation

The grizzlies of Denali Park are not very large specimens. About one-third smaller than the average grizzly bear, individuals weigh 352–473 pounds (160–216 kg). Their small size is explained by their diet, which contains insufficient meat. Here, the grizzlies eat almost nothing except plants: roots in the spring, which they dig up on tundra slopes with great dexterity; grasses in the summer, and berries in the autumn. The bears attempt to capture ground squirrels by digging around their burrows to force them to the surface and wait for them to flee, but this strategy is seldom successful. Occasionally they find a carcass. In spring the bears are able to follow the moose as they migrate to

the conifer zone to give birth and raise their young. Moose calves are also a coveted prey.

In the park the grizzly population is concentrated in the Sable Pass region, where the young are raised. They move across tundra areas covered with wild berry bushes, rocky slopes, snowfields, and riverbanks. Called "toklat," the bears that live in this region are distinguished by a lighter, sometimes blond, fur. Research shows that the female toklat often bring three young into the world, and spend three years raising them. Females with one or two young usually spend two years raising them. The bears live an average of 17 years, which is higher than the usual average of 12 years. In this part of the park, leaving the road is strictly forbidden. This rule, put in place in 1955, protects the bears' habitat and minimizes problems of human interference. Most visitors can see bears from the bus windows.

The "unkempt" look and the coloration of this grizzly are typical of the individuals in the Denali region. They are the origin of the term "grizzly," which means greyish.

Observation site

United States (Alaska): Katmai National Park

Katmai National Park was established in 1918 to protect the volcanos of the Valley of Ten Thousand Smokes. It includes 163 miles (260 km) of coastline along the Shelikof Strait, which is one-third of the coastal area extending from Cape Kubagakli to Cape Gull. It is the second most important maritime park on the continent, with 481 miles (770 km) of coastland and a surface area of 3.84 million acres (1.6 million hectares). In June 1912, the volcano at Mount Katmai and Novarupta began to erupt; a glowing stream of lava burned the entire valley for 20 miles (32 km) and covered it with ash. Mount Katmai collapsed and formed a crater. A glacier then formed along its sides—the only glacier in the world whose precise origin is known. Today, the Valley of Ten Thousand Smokes offers a lunar landscape with deep, cold lakes, volcanoes, and closed valleys.

Located at the extreme northern end of the Alaskan Peninsula, this rough territory permits the discovery of diverse wildlife. It is the largest sanctuary for grizzly bears in the United States. Several sites preserve its habitat intact, but three areas allow especially good viewing of bears fishing for salmon: Brooks Camp, coiled in the center of Katmai Park among several lakes including Lake Naknek; the McNeil River Sanctuary on the northern edge of the park; and Kodiak Island, located southeast of Katmai Park, from which it is separated by Shelikof Strait.

83

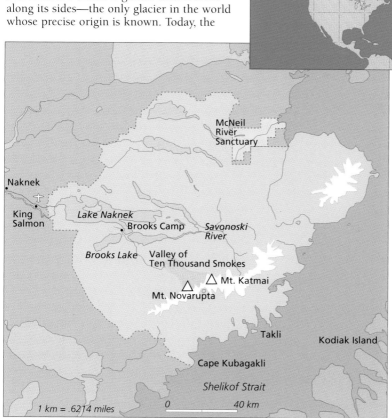

McNeil River Sanctuary

Naknek

King Salmon

Lake Naknek

Brooks Camp

Savonoski River

Brooks Lake

Valley of Ten Thousand Smokes

Mt. Novarupta

Mt. Katmai

Takli

Kodiak Island

Cape Kubagakli

Shelikof Strait

1 km = .6214 miles

0   40 km

Flora and fauna

Besides the grizzly bear, many animal species can be observed. At the end of June, the sockeye salmon, which attract bears, ospreys, and bald eagles, arrive from the ocean and swim upstream to spawn. At this time, they stop eating and their color becomes reddish, a layer of fat forms on their back, and their teeth grow longer. During the long swim upstream, the fish suffer many hardships—running against rocks, bites from other fish, and exhaustion—but that is the price of reproduction. After the eggs have been deposited, the males and females begin to undergo necrosis and their lives end at the same place they began. The salmon was the basis of the diet of local peoples for thousands of years.

The caribou herd of the Alaska Peninsula was estimated at 2,000 individuals in 1940. In 1984 the population surpassed 20,000 before settling between 15,000 and 18,000. The elk and moose inhabit dense forests and marshy areas. One must avoid females with young and males during the rutting season,

The caribou are plentiful because of the richness of this preserved region. The immensity of the park allows them to move around all year in safety from hunters.

84

The Valley of the Ten Thousand Smokes was discovered in 1910 by a National Geographic Society expedition.

The red fox often attacks burrowing rodents or ground squirrels that live in large numbers in the park in the shelter of their burrows.

at the end of August and the beginning of September, because they can prove very dangerous.

Among the park's mammals are the marten, mink, beaver, otter, and lynx. The bird world is represented by the willow ptarmigan, the black grouse, the short-eared owl, and the osprey. The bald eagle is the raptor most easily seen by park visitors. It raises its young in August and teaches them to catch the salmon that collect at the river mouths.

In spring and autumn many migratory birds assemble along the shore: ducks, geese, grebes, loons, and sandpipers. In summer, several species of seabirds nest there: kittiwakes, puffins, oyster catchers, guillemots, auks, and Bering gulls. One also can see the peregrine falcon building its nest in the cliffs.

Several species of marine mammals inhabit the coast: the Steller sea lion, whose population has declined sharply in recent decades, the seal, sea otter, walrus, rare gray whale, and the killer whale.

85

The first inhabitants of Katmai

The study of Katmai Park has contributed to a better understanding of the prehistoric culture of this part of Alaska. More than 4,000 years ago, people came to live on the Brooks River. The resources must have been abundant becaue many settled there: traces of at least ninety inhabited sites have been found.

Some lived in huts dug into the ground to protect them from the violent winds and harsh

winters; others spent the winter in the mountains, descending only in the summer and taking advantage of the massive upstream movement of the salmon. Their shelters were more spartan. Recent research has proven that these people hunted bears.

We also know from the stories of the ancient peoples that the most respected man was one who could confront a bear. Armed with a spear, he would goad the animal into charging. Then he planted his arm against the ground and waited for the animal to impale itself against the spear.

These populations also live by hunting caribou, seals, whales, wolves, and eagles; they ate several types of seabirds and mollusks that they collected in the tidal zones of the islands in Shelikof Strait.

An ancient set of trails that cross the park connected several tribes, allowing them to vary their diet and to share stories and cultures. Three sites significant to those civilizations have been identified: the Savonoski River, the Island of Takli, and the Brooks River.

The U.S. Fish and Wildlife Service is responsible for protecting 800 species of migratory birds, 600 species of threatened plants and animals, 50 species of fish, and some marine species such as the sea otter and the walrus.

Entry to Katmai is by lottery selection from all applications received. Obtain an application by written or phone request to the Alaska Department of Fish and Game, Anchorage, AK. Apply by March 1.

Observation

Unlike other national parks where the pressure of tourists is very strong (Yellowstone, Banff, and Jasper, for example), the Katmai National Park has the advantage of having preserved its ecosystem: human impact is nearly nonexistent, and the bears are numerous, constituting the most important part of the world's population of grizzlies. The density (5.76 bears per square mile, or 2.25 per square kilometer), is the highest in the world: Kodiak Island, famous

for its bears, has only 3.71 per square miles (1.45 per square kilometer) and Yellowstone only 0.26 (0.102). Although they are found in all parts of the Katmai Park, the bears often group together along the coast. They follow routes that parallel the salmon rivers and run along the lakes. These trails are very useful for walkers, but they must use necessary precautions. The best times to observe the bears are between the last week of June and the first week of August, as well as the month of September.

During the summer, the bears follow streams to feed on salmon. At the end of July, they are especially attracted by the millions of salmon that migrate from Bristol Bay toward Lake Naknek and its river network.

During this time, fish are so numerous that it is difficult to see the bottom of the stream. The generous contribution of salmon to their diet allows the Katmai bears to reach a respectable weight: the mature males may weigh as much as 900 pounds (410 kg), with the average weight falling between 396–792 pounds (180–360 kg).

86

The grizzly watches for every silvery reflection that indicates the presence of a salmon. It can remain so motionless that this photograph could be taken at a shutter speed of 1/5 second.

PRACTICAL INFORMATION

Katmai National Park is immense and wild. To discover it,
the visitor may use one of several strategies: the most common is to arrive at Brooks Camp and
plan from that point; others involve the advance planning of a route through the park.

TRANSPORTATION

The simplest route is to fly from Ancorage to King Salmon (300 miles [480 km], southwest of Anchorage), a route covered by several airlines (Mark Air, Peninsula Air, Alaska Air, and Katmai Air). A seaplane will take you from King Salmon to Brooks Camp. Several seaplane companies can land in other parts of the park.

LODGING

Brooks Camp offers two possibilities for lodging: a lodge and a campground. The lodge, which has been in use since 1950, includes 16 modern rooms for two to four people, with shower and toilet. Overlooking Lake Naknek, the lodge hangs over the famous Brooks River. A campground, located in the middle of the bear area, offers 18 campsites, each accommodating two tents and four persons. The campground is equipped with three shelters for cooking to be shared by all campers. Cooking is forbidden in all other locations. In 1995 four night-camping permits were distributed by lottery.

Brooks Camp has a store stocked with sandwiches, dehydrated and frozen food, and heating gas, but it is recommended that you bring food yourself. Some bear-proof containers are provided for storing food.

MOVING AROUND

(independently in the park)
It is absolutely necessary to obtain a visitors' permit from a park ranger and to outline your precise itinerary before going deeper into the park. You must stick to your itinerary in case you have a problem and notify park personnel of your return. The hiker must face rivers, floods, mountains, and dense forests; and there are no man-made trails, so the hiker must follow the trails established by the animals along the waterways. The best method is to plan your itinerary with park personnel at King Salmon and Brooks Camp.

CLIMATE

The climate improves between the end of May and the beginning of July. Mosquitoes are especially plentiful between June and mid-August, so hikers are a bit more comfortable later, although after the mosquitoes thin out, storms become more frequent. In mid-September the temperature drops, bringing the first snowfalls.

PLACES TO VISIT

Traditional objects of art made by the Inuit, the Aleut, and other Native Americans are sold on the outskirts of the park. The tourist center in King Salmon provides a summary of information about bears, volcanoes, marine fauna, plants, and cultural history.

Two paleontologists recently discovered that at the end of the Jurassic period (145 million years ago), Katmai was home to a species of animal very different from those that one sees there today: the *Magalneusaurus* pliosaur, a giant, 29.5-foot (9-m) marine reptile with fins, a long tail, and a neck terminating in a tapered head similar to that of a crocodile. Three deposits of remains are identified on a map exhibited at Naknek, at the entrance to Katmai National park. These promising sites will be studied, and it may be revealed that at one time today's southwest Alaska was a "Jurassic Park"! At Brooks Camp traditional houses of prehistoric native peoples have been reconstructed. They are open to the public.

Educational Programs

In the summer Katmai National Park offers a variety of free activities that promote better understanding of the natural and cultural resources of the region. Slide shows, guided hikes, and conferences are organized by the park's naturalists and guides.

RECOMMENDATIONS

You are in bear country and must submit to strict rules. All visitors arriving at Brooks Camp are requested to report to the visitors' center to receive a short briefing on bears and to learn the proper approach for a region they inhabit. This program answers many questions about the animal and gives a fairly good idea of the rules that must be followed at Katmai. A ten-minute video provides information about the protection of bears and of humans. After this educational session, you will be given a badge to be worn for the duration of your stay in the park.

Some important rules to follow: when bears are present, remain between the platforms and the Brooks River; use the campsites provided (reservation necessary). Picnics are forbidden on the Brooks River and on the beach of Lake Naknek, which is located 2,620 feet (800 m) from the river.

87

The Polar Bear
(Ursus maritimus)

Double page preceding. A female and her 10-month-old cub moving toward the shore of Hudson Bay. Interrupted by naps and nursing, the journey will be long before reaching the first seal hunting on the ice floe.

In summer the tundra offers little potential prey to the polar bears. Seals are inaccessible and the large ungulates are wary; only the lemmings and coveys of snow geese are on the menu.

90

Description

Average length: Adult male, 7.9–8.5 feet (240–260 cm); adult female, 6.2–6.9 feet (190–210 cm).
Shoulder height: Adults, 3.3–4 feet (1–1.2 m).
Weight: Adult male, 660–1,600 pounds (300–730 kg); adult female, 216–990 pounds (98–450 kg), depending on the season; newborn, 15.8–28 ounces (450–800 gr). Females feed their young for an extremely long time; their weight may vary by 50 percent between the time they enter the den and the time they leave.

Polar bears' dominant color is white, but varies from yellow to deep orange depending on location and season. These variations are due to the oxidation of fats and the dirt that accumulates in the fur during the summer. In winter the bears are pure white because they can scrub themselves against the snow and ice. The rear part of the body is higher than the shoulders. The neck, long and flattened on the vertical surfaces, supports a comparatively small head. The muzzle is black. The claws, which are powerful, are short and curved. The tail and outer ears are quite small.

Habitat

The polar bear is confined to ice floes and the coasts of the Arctic regions. It does not occupy a particular territory, but moves across the wide spaces of a landscape constantly shaped by violent winds, water currents, and tides.

Movement

The polar bear moves continuously in search of the best seal-hunting areas. Bear populations follow the seasonal changes in ice floes in a movement that could be classified as migration. The bears usually remain on the ice close to the most broken coastline, which is the habitat preferred by seals. When it walks, a polar bear moves at an average speed of 2.5 miles (4 km) per hour, but when pursued by a hunter it can attain a speed of nearly 22 miles (35 km) per hour for a short distance.

Food

The diet of the polar bear consists mainly of harp seals. However, it also hunts other species of marine mammals, such as the bearded seal and the walrus. In the summer, the period of food shortage, the bear is satisfied with carrion, baby ducks, shore birds, algae, and other plants.

The polar bear is the only true carnivore of the bear family, as evidenced by its dental structure. Its premolars are much sharper than those of its relatives that eat roots and berries. The polar bear is a hunter with strategies that vary according to location, weather conditions, and the type of prey sought. It never tracks seals in the water, waiting patiently instead near the seal's breathing hole, then sliding along the ice or swimming along a channel to approach its prey. In the winter it kills sturgeon when the fish are forced to congregate in small areas of open water.

92

A polar bear's life is harsh and unpredictable. The sea ice may be frozen solid in cold, calm weather and broken during storms.

Predators

The only true predator of this species is man. No observation has confirmed the predation of killer whales on polar bears. Occasionally, wolves attack a female bear with young of three to four months. Some of the bear's prey, such as the walrus, may kill a bear in defending themselves.

Longevity

Polar bears have two especially critical periods of life: their departure from the maternal den, when they are exposed for the first time to the rigors of the Arctic, and separation from their mother, when they must first hunt alone. The adult bear may have to deal with famine, the risk of drowning, and exposure to certain diseases. However, in general, the adult bear has a long life expectancy of up to thirty years for males and as much as forty years for females in captivity.

Maturity

Females reach maturity at age four to five and males at age three. However, the shoulders of the male are not wide enough for mating until age eight to ten.

Range

The polar bear is dispersed around the Arctic Circle and has been observed at 88 degrees north latitude and southern colonies on James and Hudson Bays. Before the arrival of Europeans, the bear occupied a wider range, reaching Nova Scotia. Several observations also place the bear as far as Kamchatka and the Commander Islands in the North Pacific.

The polar bear is extremely curious and does not hesitate to venture near inhabited areas. This character trait has brought it many difficulties with man.

Population

In 1993 the world population was estimated at between 21,000 and 28,000 individuals, showing a steady increase according to geographic area.

History

For thousands of years, the bear knew only human Arctic enemies armed with spears and bows. The Chukchis and the Nenets hunted the bear for its meat and skin, its especially solid bones, and its fat. They also hunted it because the bear, so close to themselves, was a symbol of power and virility. When whale hunters and explorers arrived, the number of bears killed increased rapidly. In the fifteenth century, whale hunters began to navigate in the arctic regions seeking right whales. They were followed by adventurers in quest of navigation routes connecting with the spice routes to China. Impressed by the harshness and wildness of the region, they systematically killed all the bears they encountered. Bearskins and live animals were given as gifts to royalty and church officials. The Viking leader Eric the Red is said to have sent polar bear pelts as gifts to the rulers of Egypt. Later, the polar bear was hunted for its other by-products. On the island of Svalbard, Russian and then Norwegian trappers massacred tens of thousands of polar bears by trapping and poisoning them. Beginning at the end of the nineteenth century, virtual polar safaris accelerated the disappearance of the largest carnivore. Attracted by burned seal fat, the bears came to the ships and were massacred. After World War II, the Arctic became more accessible. By the 1950s, big game hunters armed with high velocity rifles arrived in the Arctic to kill polar bears. "Hunts," viewed by some as "slaughters," were organized by helicopter. Specific legislation in 1965 by the International Union for the Conservation of Nature and Natural Resources (IUCN) declared the polar bear as endangered and steps were taken to ensure its survival. In the 1970s, the population fell to a minimum of around 10,000, perhaps less. International research

93

In early November, the bears congregate at Cape Churchill to wait for Hudson Bay to freeze.

cooperation and the passage of specific legislation brought an end to this decline. Today, it is the bear's habitat that is threatened, with the establishment of a satellite-launching base at Churchill and oil exploration in northern Alaska.

Life cycle

The life cycle of the polar bear is quite different from that of other bears. Female polar bears begin to breed at four or five years of age. Since each female will have only 8 cubs during her life, she can be choosy about which male to mate with. In autumn, around early November, the pregnant female digs a den in the first snow. This site is chosen carefully for its snow, which must be firm but not too hard, and for its auspicious location for capturing the warmth of the sun beginning in early March. In some locations the female digs in permafrost; in others she lies down on a slope and allows herself to be covered by snow. The den consists of an access corridor, a main chamber, and sometimes smaller annex chambers. The cavern is about 9 degrees F above the outside temperature and is linked to the outside world by a ventilation shaft. The chamber is always above the shaft to ensure that warm air is kept inside. During this period the males, immature bears, and females with cubs spend the winter and the spring seeking breaks in the ice where seals can be found. In one year they may cover hundreds of miles over a surface equal to half that of France. If food is scarce, they may also spend part of the winter in a hole in the snow.

Between December 15 and January 15, the female gives birth to an average of two young, which are covered with a fine down, are blind, and weigh barely 21 ounces (600 gr). The family leaves its shelter between March 15 and April 15, depending on the latitude. The female gradually introduces her cubs to the rigors of the Arctic. She begins by partially removing the snow blocking the passage to the outside, allowing cool air to enter the den. After they have spent several days discovering the snow, the cold, and the environs, the young follow their mother toward the ice floe, sometimes a walk of several miles.

The family den remains sealed for two years. The cubs must learn from their mother how to hunt seals,

94

Nonmating males spend their time playing or jousting in preparation for the combat that they will have to endure in order to mate.

find their way in a labyrinth of ice, and protect themselves during a blizzard, in short, to become the largest predators of the Arctic. When the female decides that her offspring have attained the necessary weight and independence, she drives them away. Then she signals her availability for mating by leaving a scent. Several adult males locate and follow this trail. It is at this time that the size and corpulence of the suitors is important, because they may have to fight for the right to approach the female, and the biggest is most likely to win.

Mating occurs in the spring, in April or May. After spending a week with a male, the female pushes him away. Then males and females take advantage of the last weeks of ice to gain weight. Unlike other bears, the polar bear's time of food scarcity is the summer. When the ice floe has disappeared, the bears move onto land, moving slowly to save their reserves and taking long rests. Depending on the region, they resume their seal hunting in October or November.

Indications of presence

Compared to other bears, the polar bear's presence is less obvious. The main sign of a bear's passing through is the footprint. A trail left behind the hind feet indicates the passage of a large male with long fur on its feet; smaller trails left beside, with smaller footprints, are an unmistakable sign of a female with cubs. However, in deep snow the young follow their mother very closely, and their tracks may disappear. Sometimes the

wind makes old footprints reappear as it blows powder around a pile of snow made by the animal.

In bad weather and strong wind, the bear digs a quick shelter into which it wedges itself against a block of snow; scratched and piled snow shows the imprint of the predator's body and indicates its passage. The killing of a seal leaves significant remains. The leftover meat attracts scavengers, and a flock of large crows above an ice floe indicates the presence of a carcass, or even of a bear finishing its meal.

In the summer, in unsettled moraine regions, observers must be careful because the indications are less visible, and the bears are warmer and wander less. They may dig a hollow in the permafrost, and nothing resembles a rock more than a perfectly still, dirty bear rolled into a ball. In March a family den can be identified by the scratchings of the female as she searches for lichens. Traces of urine and small stripped saplings indicate a play area and a nearby den.

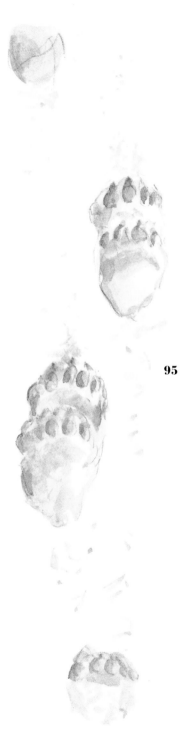

95

Observation site

Canada (Manitoba): Churchill

Located at 59 degrees north latitude on Hudson Bay, the Churchill region is unique because it is the intersection of three distinct habitats: tundra, northern forest, and sea. About two million years ago, it was covered by a glacier that melted only 8,000 years ago. The melting caused the emergence of the land masses that form what today is Cape Churchill and the surrounding area. Boat mooring rings installed at the beginning of the eighteenth century at Sloop's Cove are now several meters above the water level, signs of the continual rising of the land.

The soil is in a state of intermittent permafrost. A large number of shallow lakes 2 feet to 3.1 feet (60 cm–1 cm) deep are favorable habitat for mosquitoes, which are abundant in summer, and for birds. From Cape Merry to Bird Cove, the coastal landscape is marked by many outcroppings

of white rock, formed from quartzite dating from the Precambrian period. Various glacial flows have eroded these rocks and marked them with parallel striations. The first people to settle there, around 1700 B.C., belonged to the nomadic pre-Dorset civilization. They occupied the region until 900 B.C., when they were supplanted by the Dorsets, who were technologically more advanced and closer to the present-day Inuit, but who themselves were replaced by a people called the Thule about the year 1000. Beginning in 1100, various peoples who survive today began to share the Churchill region. Today's population is composed of native Cree from the south, Denes from the west, Inuit from the north, European Americans, and people of mixed race.

In the 1930s, the construction of a grain elevator and a railroad supply line gave the town of Churchill a new purpose. People's heads were turned by the dream of an Arctic metropolis of 30,000 inhabitants. In 1950 the city was rebuilt outside the shoreline, in its present location. Until 1956 public services were administered by the major

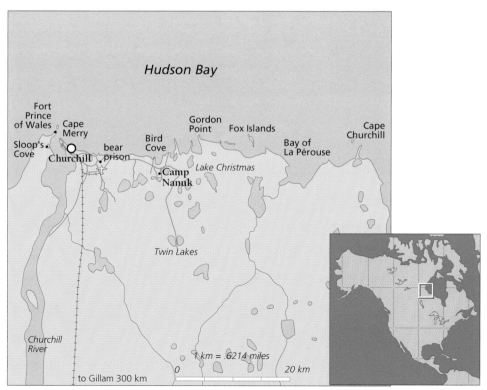

military base nearby. Its closure brought the construction of a model complex that included a hospital, school, ice rink, library, cafeteria, and environmental-services office. The names of the streets running at right angles recall the eventful history of the conquest of Canada: Hudson, La Perouse, Kelsey, Munk.

Flora and fauna

In October, when the bears are present, the summer fauna has already disappeared. The 3,500 sturgeon and 200 species of nesting birds have left for more comfortable wintering places. Some snow buntings are still flying in clouds at ground level. The gyrfalcon and the goshawk may still be present at the beginning of November. In winter the willow ptarmigan and rock ptarmigan peck together at willow shoots. The snowy owl, often seen perched on an electric pole or large rock, waits for a lemming to pass by. The Arctic fox, in its white winter coat, searches constantly along the beaches and among the stones for a rodent or the carcass of a bird. Sometimes a crossed fox, a variant form of the red fox with a black cross on the shoulders, conceals itself in the coastal grass. The tundra, so colorful in summer, is gray and brown now. The willows take on a magenta hue.

Beginning with the first snows, the larch branches fold under the added weight.

Sparse spruces are characteristic of regions with a very harsh climate. The largest branches are at the base, where they are protected all winter by the snow.

Observation

Observation of polar bears at Churchill presents no difficulty. Every year the Hudson Bay population makes a migration as precise as a clock's movement. In July, when the ice floes break up, the population moves onto land around Cape Tatnam. It goes northward up the coast, reaching Cape Churchill in October (some bears are already seen there in July). The only cape on the west coast of the bay, Churchill stops the blocks of ice that are pushed in that direction by the prevailing winds. Besides that, the fresh water brought

97

In October the snowy owl takes advantage of the last snowless days to feed on small tundra mammals before continuing its flight south.

The Polar Bear Capital of the World

The first information about the Churchill region dates from 1619, when the Danish navigator Jens Munk, overwintering under the worst possible conditions, believed that he had arrived at one of the entrances to the much-sought Northwest Passage.

In 1688, after several visits to the mouth of the Churchill River, the Hudson's Bay Company (ironically nicknamed "Here Before the Christ"

because it arrived in the region so early) decided to establish a base for hunting sturgeon, which were numerous in the estuary in the summer.

In 1774 Samuel Hearne came to govern Fort Prince of Wales. A very adventurous person, he crossed the Canadian north to the ocean, guided by a native. He left fascinating notes

The end of October is the best time to see the bears. On Halloween night, while the children are running around the streets asking for treats, it is not rare to see bears approach the doors of houses. And it is not the traditional pumpkin that scares them away . . .

about a place where polar bears gave birth, a place that still exists, about 31 miles (50 km) from the town.

The establishment of a company trading post at Hudson Bay attracted the native population of Cree and Denes, whose descendants still inhabit the small town of Churchill.

Hunters exchanged bearskins (especially those of the black bear) and beaver and fox pelts for English merchandise.

This activity was still going on in the 1950s. For several decades, the presence of a training ground for the Canadian army made people forget about the bear population. No study was made of the possible impact of the military presence on the life cycle of the bears, their population, and their migratory path in the region.

In 1964 the departure of the military and the establishment of the international charter protected the polar bear over its entire range, fortunately allowing the population to recover.

It was Charles Jonkel, an eminent specialist in North American bears, who was the first to become interested in this population in 1966. Repeated accidents and numerous killings by bears who were defending themselves led to the establishment of safety measures, the construction of the bear prison (1981), and the creation of a surveillance patrol.

The increasing presence of bears around Halloween at the Churchill garbage dump began to attract visitors and reporters. In 1979 an ingenious mechanic, Len Smith, built a truck chassis capable of moving tourists and photographers, anxious to see bears in their natural habitat, across the tundra with a certain amount of comfort.

Stories in *Life* and *National Geographic* made the place famous. The dump is now off-limits for bears, and any bear that breaks the rule is driven off or tranquilized and placed in one of the 16 cells of the prison. In some cases, the bears are killed (two or three yearly). Thus, the "Polar Bear Capital of the World" was born.

PRACTICAL INFORMATION

Do not plan on visiting the bear prison; it is off-limits to all visitors.

TRANSPORTATION

■ **BY AIR.** The town of Churchill is accessible by air (Canadian airlines) from Winnipeg (a flight of one hour and 45 minutes) with a stopover at Gilliam or Thompson.

■ **BY TRAIN.** Trains depart from Winnipeg, but you should expect the round trip to take 72 hours.

■ **BY CAR.** It is possible to rent a car locally or a snowmobile in winter when the snow cover is sufficient.

DISTANCES

From Churchill to Winnipeg (by railroad): 1,000 miles (1,600 km)
From Churchill to LePas (by railroad): 513 miles (821 km)

LODGING

During the period when bear viewing is best, the lodging places are fully booked. The hotels and guest houses are reserved several years in advance by Canadian and American companies. Thus, it is quite difficult for an individual to get to Churchill and obtain a place on a tundra vehicle. Individuals and couples usually join a group of thirty American tourists.

CLIMATE

The general climate of the region is considered subarctic, strongly influenced by maritime air masses. The average precipitation is 16 inches (400 m). The prevailing winds are from the northwest. In recent times, the climate may vary so that conditions are quite different from one year to the next. For example, on October 30, 1993, the temperature was 1.4 degrees F (–17 degrees C); on the same date the following year the thermometer showed 34 degrees F (1 degree C). Snowfalls generally are limited.

At times storms with violent winds change the weather quickly; otherwise conditions are often stable, with lead-gray skies and "mild" temperatures of 32 to 23 degrees F (0 to –5 degrees C).

PLACE TO VISIT

The Churchill Museum, run by missionaries of the congregation of Oblates of the Immaculate Virgin, houses one of Canada's richest collections of objects from the pre-Dorset and Dorset civilizations (1700 B.C. to A.D. 1000). The Dorset culture was followed by that of the Thules, then by the Caribou Eskimos. The Inuit of the eighteenth and nineteenth centuries left circles of stones to mark the perimeter of their tents, fox traps, and caches of meat that are still visible on the peninsula to the west of the estuary. The services of Park Canada have organized a small exhibit on the history of the Hudson's Bay Company and the trade between the natives and the Europeans. In summer one can also view films on the bear and on the region and its history. Cape Merry offers a good view of the estuary of the Churchill River, an important

site in the region's history. A battery of cannons remains that was never used because its planners never considered that Fort Prince of Wales is exactly in its line of fire on the opposite bank. Built by the English between 1731 and 1771 using rock found on site, the fort was destroyed by La Perouse in 1782. Environment Canada has restored it for visitors (it is only open in the summer). Watch out for bears.

RECOMMENDATIONS

On visits to the tundra by truck, the motor must be turned off when bears are present. Windows may be rolled down for better viewing. A tank mounted on the rear of the truck allows a maximum of four persons to remain outside (this is reserved for those who are not sensitive to the cold!).

99

Willow ptarmigan are birds that spend the winter in polar regions. They feed on small plants that they find in patches of ground where the wind has removed the snow.

You are prohibited from leaving the truck and approaching bears or running after grouse or fox. You are also completely forbidden to feed the animals; failure to comply results in your tour organizer forfeiting his license.

by the Churchill and Seal Rivers reduces the bay's salinity and promotes its freezing. These two factors favor the presence of bears who are impatient to resume their seal hunt on the ice floes. The most favorable time to see them is quite short, between the last six days of October and the first five days of November. Contrary to old reports that have been recorded too many times, bears are no longer seen at the dumps that were located at the edge of town.

The best way to view the bears is to use the services of local tour organizers. In fact,

who is mentioned in the *Guinness Book of World Records* as the man who has captured the most polar bears—the helicopter allows you to see the ice floe as it is being formed, and the bears of Cape Churchill and Fox Island, which often are among the largest males. Sometimes it also is possible to see a fox or a caribou that has been left behind. In 1996 a chartered helicopter cost 800 Canadian dollars for one hour for four persons. Polar bear sightings are usually guaranteed.

Another viewing area is the polar bear "prison," a large hangar-like compound near the airport where dangerous bears are kept until released safely.

Infrequent in October, the aurora borealis is quite visible in March and April.

The aurora borealis

The aurora borealis takes its name from the Roman goddess of dawn. The effect is strongest two days after intense solar activity, the time it takes the wind's radiation to reach the earth from the sun. The aurora phenomenon can only be seen on a moonless night with a clear sky. It may appear at any time but, considering its faint light, requires excellent conditions of darkness to be seen. The aurora australis (of the south) is distinguished from the aurora borealis (of the north) only by its name; the phenomena are identical. They are initiated by the introduction of charged particles into atmospheric layers, following the lines of the earth's magnetic field.

the use of special tundra buses is indispensable. At that time of year the soil is frozen, but moving across it is slow and difficult. Reservations for lodging must be made more than a year in advance. Visits are very highly valued by American and Canadian tourists, and it is preferable to avoid joining one of their groups, which are too large and often too noisy.

Photographers choose buses that hold a large number of riders so that everyone can get a clear view. One method of discovery that should not be neglected: the helicopter. Piloted by a specialist—such as Steve Miller,

These particles come from the "solar" wind, a continuous displacement of particles emanating from the sun, which distort the earth's magnetic field. The effects are many: radioelectrical, magnetic, and, especially, luminous. For hours at a time, magnificent greenish-yellow folds furrow the heavens. These magnetic storms are not regular, but are produced sporadically, like rainstorms. In October the cycles of the sun's activity always create an intense period in which the chances of observation of this marvelous phenomenon are quite good. March and April are also potentially good viewing times.

100

Canada (Ontario): James Bay

Polar Bear Provincial Park was established in April 1970 to protect the summer habitat of the polar bear on the northwest coast of James Bay and the south coast of Hudson Bay, at 54 degrees north latitude and 87 degrees west longitude. This territory is a region of arctic and subarctic landscapes in one of the parts of Ontario least affected by civilization. The coastal fringe of the park extends from the west bank of the James Bay to the area of Fort Severn, which is located about 60 miles (100 km) from the Manitoba border. The park has a surface area of 9,413 square miles (24,097 square km), about four times the area of Banff National Park, but it is visited very little (only 600 persons per year, compared with the millions who visit

Banff). As protected land, the park can be traversed only along the walking paths and by canoe trips along the Winish, Sutton, and Shagamu Rivers. Campsites are limited. In fact, the populated places see themselves as cultural conservation points for the native populations whose ancestral way of life has undergone radical changes. One of the most visited areas, located to the south and west of Winisk, is for natives who cannot be away from their homes for a long period of time. Abandoned shelters in the park can now be visited for their historical interest.

The James Bay territory is home to some 6,000 Cree, members of an Algonquin Indian tribe. They rebelled against the damming of the rivers by the planned hydro-electric plant since they believed that only beavers should build dams.

101

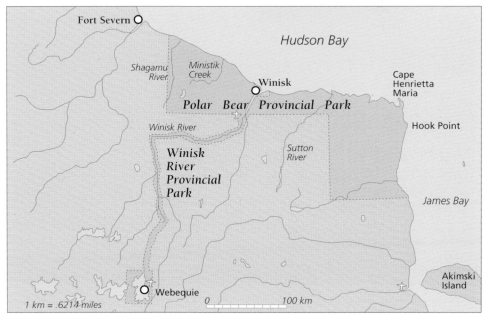

Fort Severn

Hudson Bay

Shagamu River

Ministik Creek

Winisk

Cape Henrietta Maria

Polar Bear Provincial Park

Winisk River

Hook Point

Winisk River Provincial Park

Sutton River

James Bay

Webequie

Akimski Island

1 km = .6214 miles

0   100 km

Flora and fauna

The park's vegetation is characterized by a tundra zone and a zone of northern forest where the climate permits only minimal tree growth. The park is divided by the northern edge of the forest, where white and black pine, larch, and balsam grow. In the tundra zone, sprinkled with marshes and shallow lakes, permafrost and peat bogs create a terrain favorable for the growth of moisture-loving vegetation. Black bear, red fox, wolves, lynx, otters, beavers, wolverines, muskrats, skunks, and elk make up the fauna of the northern forest.

The arctic fox, the arctic hare, and herds of caribou—of which 350 congregate regularly near Hook Point—

The caribou make long migratory treks along the coast.

102

Polar Bear Provincial Park is creased by wide deltas coming from rivers that have crossed Ontario to empty into James Bay.

The Cree and the Hudson's Bay Company

Beginning at the end of the seventeenth century, French and English adventurers engaged in fur trade with the natives of the region, the Cree. The first trading post, Fort Albany, was established at the mouth of the Albany River. When the trading posts of the Hudson's Bay Company were established, contemporary records show that the demand for skins grew, especially for those of the black and grizzly bears. Most of the native hunters kept the precious, lush hair of the polar bear for their own personal use. The price for a polar bear skin was 40 percent less than that for a brown or black bear. The fur trade caused the reorganization of other native peoples and Inuit families located near the trading posts. Fortunately, the natives were able to preserve their traditions despite these developments.

The bear hunt has always had a dominant place in the Cree culture, and represents a mixture of faith and pragmatism. The hunt is embedded in a ceremonial rite symbolizing the rebirth of the animal killed in the hunt. The hunter could use several methods to find a bear's den: following fresh tracks to the den in autumn, examining old shelters and possible places of refuge, or relying on premonitory dreams, like the Cree who hunted along James Bay in the pine forests: "I saw myself at the den of Memekwesiw, and I thought that the door was a stone. The body and face of the spirit of the bears was covered with hair. There were many trees around us, and it said to me, 'This is where my young bear is,' showing me the place. The next day I put on my new gloves and headed for the place it had shown me. The bear really was there."

Some days before leaving, the hunter sings, accompanied by his drum, about the events to follow. He never speaks the true name of the bear, but calls it "cousin," "grandmother," "son of the chief," "the man with four paws," or "the young of Memekwesiw." The night before, he cleanses himself by taking a bath and prepares his most beautiful hunting clothes while the camp is being cleaned. Then he goes, without stopping along the way, to the den. There, he examines the breathing hole. If it is yellow all around, the bear is inside. If not, he pushes a stick into the hole to verify. He calls the bear by its name, asking it to come out. The bear growls, the hunter calls it again, then the bear comes out and charges. The hunter strikes it in the head with a harpoon, which makes it easier to tell whether the bear is dead than if he attacked it with arrows or a gun. Then, with the dead bear, the hunter returns in silence to his camp. Following the prescribed ritual, the feast begins. The head is eaten first, then the front paws, then the rest is shared among all the members of the tribe. To be healed, a sick or wounded person is allowed to have the part of the bear that corresponds to the affected part of the body.

103

inhabit the tundra. The bird population of the northern regions includes 300 species.

This is an important migration route for many ducks, geese, and swans (Canada goose, snow goose, pintail, teal, black duck, goldeneye, whistling swan, and oldsquaw). The rich intertidal zone of James Bay attracts the arctic and common loons, the red-necked phalarope, the greater and lesser yellowlegs, and the Hudsonian godwit.

The willow ptarmigan and the snowy owl inhabit the tundra, while songbirds remain for a time in the northern forest before resuming their journey. The waters of James Bay are hospitable to the sturgeon that congregate in large numbers in the summer. Walrus and seals also frequent this region. Fishermen consider the trout caught in the rivers affected by tides here among the best in the world.

At the tip of James Bay, the forest gives way to the taiga vegetative zone. The true tundra is much farther north, well beyond any road access. Polar bears, woodland caribou and white whales can be seen during spring and summer. Other mammals include

seal, silver and arctic fox, timber wolf, otter and beaver. Water fowl species include Snow and Canada geese and many duck species.

Observation

The best time to visit the park is between the end of July and the end of August, both for viewing bears and because of the weather. Later in the season, fog and violent winds impede free movement.

The polar bear population of James Bay, the southernmost of the species, is estimated at only 700 individuals. The eastern part of Hudson Bay is home to another thousand. The first visitors noted the presence of family groups, as did maps of the seventeenth century that referred to Akimski Island and the Twin Island (in James Bay) as "the cubs." For a period of two years, the females follow an elliptical path within the bay. A region of dens has been identified on Akimski Island, and others have been dug in the back country of Ministik Creek and along the Shagamu

104

In the summer the ice has disappeared and the bears move along the coast in search of a beached whale or a seal. They bathe regularly during the hottest days.

River. It also seems that the archipelago of the Belcher Islands is a favorable place for establishing maternal caves. The natives of the region still hunt bears occasionally.

In the summer, when the sea ice breaks up, the bears must move to land. The first sightings may be made in the first week of July. At the end of the month, more bears have arrived between Winisk and Fort Severn. Others congregate in large numbers at Cape Henrietta Maria and in the region of the Pen Islands. Small groups are also seen south of

Hook Point. In August and September, some individuals move along the coast of Hudson Bay toward the northwest.

The best way to locate groups of polar bears along the coast is by seaplane. A permit is required to charter a seaplane. Beginning in the month of November, with the formation of ice floes, the bears turn back to the north. They may go as far as 375 miles (600 km) away, crossing the 60th parallel. In February, in midwinter, they have moved an average of 173 miles (278 km) from the coast.

PRACTICAL INFORMATION

Every year 600 visitors discover Polar Bear Provincial Park.

TRANSPORTATION

■ **BY AIR.** By commercial airline, fly to Toronto and then to Thunder Bay. An airline company carries passengers as far as Webequie. Seaplanes serve the villages farther to the north of the park.

A permit is required to charter a plane; it can be obtained from the Ministry of Natural Resources at Moosonee. The landing areas in the park are limited.

DISTANCES

From Winisk to Moosonee: 342 miles (547 km)
From Winisk to Toronto: 804 miles (1,287 km)

MOVING AROUND

Travel by boat on the James and Hudson Bays must be done with great care. Floating logs make navigation difficult, the low-lying coastland makes marches a problem, and the weather can change abruptly. Communication is impossible, even by radio.

LODGING

Camping requires a permit, and campers must bring in all necessary provisions. They can be bought at the store in

Moosonee or Peawanuck, but you must inquire in advance about the availability of merchandise.

CLIMATE

The climate is severe: the summers are short and the weather changes fast. The temperature can plummet from 82 to 38 degrees F (28–3 degrees C) in the space of less than one hour when the wind changes direction. When the wind dies down, mosquitoes proliferate. Banks of fog coming in from the sea often spread several miles inland.

PLACES TO VISIT

Thunder Bay, located on the coast of Lake Superior, is an obligatory stopping place when traveling into northern Ontario. There the visitor will find places of great interest that will enhance the discovery of Canada's northern regions. In the region of Thunder Bay, old Fort William, located on the Kaministiquia River, was a rest stop for travelers and trappers of the seventeenth century who traded in furs. Today, the fort has been reconstructed to include 42 buildings that show the daily

life at the beginning of the 1800s.

The railroad line called the Polar Bear Express brings passengers through lakes and forests to the town of Moosonee. From there a boat takes them to Moose Factory. Established 300 years ago, this settlement served as a permanent fur-trading post for the Hudson's Bay Company. It is the oldest settlement in Ontario. A museum traces the history of traps and snowshoes and the craft of working elk skin. At Moosonee one may also take a canoe to Fossil Island, where there are fossils of the Devonian period (350 million years ago).

RECOMMENDATIONS

The resources and riches of the park are extremely delicate. Any damage or modification of the environment is an infringement of park regulations.

105

Observation site

Canada (Baffin Island): Auyuittuq National Park and surrounding areas

Auyuittuq National Park is the land of eternal ice: its name means "the place that never melts." Located on the east coast of Baffin Island, most of the park's surface is covered by the Penny Glacial Cap. Here, nature, conditioned by the ice, takes brutal forms: dizzying precipices, wild fjords, rocks broken by frost, glacial valleys shrouded in fog. The park's reserve was established in 1972 to protect the northern region of Davis, where numerous cirques, moraines, valleys, and glaciers form a unique geomorphic combination.

The park has a surface area of 8,398 square miles (21,500 square km). It contains especially well-known sites such as the majestic Overlord Peak, which guards the entrance to Pangnirtung Pass; Crater Lake, which has an intensely blue color and features a dike that was formed by a glacial moraine; the Schwartzenbach Falls, which descend 2,165 feet (660 m) into the Weasel River; and Mount Thor, named for the Scandinavian god of thunder, which has the longest continuous cliff in the world.

Baffin Land has been inhabited for 4,000 years by various groups able to adapt to the rigors of the climate. One cannot visit without making a detour to Broughton Island. Its Inuit name, Qikiqtarjuaq, means "large island"; it is 10 miles (16 km) long and 7.5 miles (12 km) wide. The highest peak, 1,942 feet (592 m) overhangs 35 miles (56 km) of coastline.

In 1956–57 the Inuit of Pangnirtung and Clyde River were moved to Broughton Island, then a store of the Hudson's Bay Company opened in 1960. Today, 95 percent of the island's inhabitants are Inuit.

106

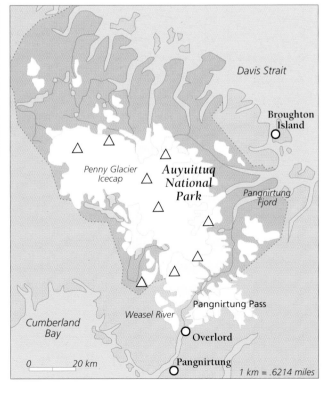

Davis Strait

Broughton Island

Penny Glacier Icecap

Auyuittuq National Park

Pangnirtung Fjord

Pangnirtung Pass

Cumberland Bay

Weasel River

Overlord

0   20 km

Pangnirtung

1 km = .6214 miles

Flora and fauna

The arctic ecosystem at Auyuittuq is
especially well adapted to the environment.
The flowers are able to resist the biting cold
and the very violent winds. They begin to
bloom in June in startling colored carpets of
violet, yellow, and white. The plants of the
arctic grow in dense tufts or in mounds to
conserve heat and avoid the wind. The only
trees able to resist the wind's effects are the
dwarf birch and the arctic willow. The latter
is the largest tree of the tundra; usually
growing at ground level, it never exceeds a
few inches in height. The Inuit call it "the
tongue plant," and they eat its leaves, which
are rich in vitamin C. The arctic eriophorum,
which produces a distinctive fluffy ball, is
adapted to damp, swampy locales. The large-
leafed willow-herb expands its rose and
purple colors.

Near the bottom of the food chain, the
lemming is an essential element. The most
common species is the snow lemming, which
is rusty brown in the summer. The lemming
populations vary considerably from one year

The northern fulmar often nests in rocky
crevices. It stays in the cliffs for protection
against arctic foxes.

Remains of the last glacial periods, glaciers hurtle down steep slopes and hew the land before
dropping into the sea.

to another, which has a direct impact on the populations of many other species that feed on them, such as the snowy owl and the arctic fox. The arctic hare lives between Lake Windy and Summit Lake. Its winter fur was used as camouflage by the Inuit, to make their kayaks look like icebergs as they hunted seals. The arctic fox is an opportunistic hunter that can feed on lemmings, the eggs and hatchlings of seabirds, or the leftovers from the meals of the polar bears that it follows. The caribou's feet are adapted to a terrain that is spongy in the summer and icy in the winter; it is smaller in size than caribou that live in the forest, and two layers of fur insulate it from the cold. The caribou was and remains heavily used by the

In mid-August the dwarf willows form a reddish carpet. Reduced to the size of bonsai, they grow very slowly.

108

The polar bear and the Inuit

The polar bear and the peoples of the north have shared the arctic for about 30,000 years. When the first people arrived from Central Asia on the coast of the Arctic Ocean, they discovered a type of bear with which they were not familiar. Confronted with the same problems as they were, the bear had developed similar solutions: it found shelter in the winter in a dug-in hut or in an ice igloo, and it fed on a unique type of game, the seal. Were the humans imitating the bear?

In the hunt, the polar men also used the bear's techniques: lie in wait close to the breathing hole in the winter, or approach slowly, crawling along the ice, in the spring. The similarities were such that the men saw the bear as a parent that they venerated when it did them the honor of visiting them after its death. To wear pants of bearskin meant to be protected effectively from the cold, but beyond that it symbolized the honor of having been accorded the fur of this king of the ice. Thus, the polar bear was omnipresent in the beliefs of the arctic peoples. From the Samoyeds of the Taymir Peninsula through the Chukchis of East Siberia to the Inuit of Thule (Greenland), all honored the bear in their own fashion. However, with the advent of firearms, the bear hunt changed

from a fratricidal, face-to-face combat to a chase in which only the tracking process recalled the ancestral relations of these two superpredators of the Arctic.

PRACTICAL INFORMATION

Access to the park is difficult.
Visitors must explore it independently, without guides.

TRANSPORTATION

■ **BY AIR.** Canadian companies serve Auyuittuq from Montreal, Ottawa, and Yellowknife. First Air Limited or Air Baffin provide flights from Iqaluit to Broughton Island or Pangnirtung.

■ **OTHER TRANSPORTATION.** Local companies provide transportation between Pangnirtung or Broughton Island and Auyuittuq by boat or by snowmobile, depending on the season. If weather conditions do not permit boat travel, it is possible to reach the park by foot, a trip of 18 miles (30 km). The trail is marked by *inukshuks*, small mounds of stone placed atop a large rock. The markings also show the best places to cross streams and prevent tundra damage.

DISTANCES

From Broughton to Iqaluit: 321 miles (513 km)
From Broughton to Pangnirtung: 141 miles (225 km)
From Broughton to the Arctic Circle: 60 miles (96 km)
From Broughton to Kivitoo: 40 miles (64 km)
From Broughton to Padloping Island: 60 miles (96 km)

LODGING

On Broughton Island, a hotel built in 1990 near the harbor has ten guest rooms. A campground provides accommodations close to the airport and the town. A nearby stream offers fresh water.

Some cabins have been built in Auyuittuq Park at a distance of one's days walk to serve as a refuge in case of problems. Hikers can camp there or wherever else they like; no route is prescribed.

CLIMATE

Between December and March, the temperature may drop to –40 degrees Celsius. Beginning at the end of June and the beginning of July, there are several weeks of twenty-four-hour sunlight. The temperature then varies between 36 and 46 degrees F (2–8 degrees C). The ice leaves Broughton Island between July 15 and July 31 and forms again at the end of October.

PLACES TO VISIT

Boat trips can be organized with a local guide to visit Davis Strait, Cape Hooper, the Pangnirtung Fjord, and the Cape Dyer region. Two hours by boat from Pangnirtung is Kekerten Historical Park, a former nineteenth-century whaling station that has been partially restored. Americans and Scots hunted right whales until the 1920s, by which time they had been depleted drastically. At the highest point on the island, a telescope allows you to exmaine the whales.

On Broughton Island, hiking trails lead you through a splendid arctic landscape. One of them goes to the site of the former village, located 13 miles (20 km) from the existing one. The route moves along unusual quartz crystal formations. On Broughton Island, many Inuit sculpt scenes from their daily life from soapstone. Some of these are expert sculptors, who make their livelihood by selling their work to tourists. To get a wider view of the island, climb onto the granite outcropping near the village, marked by an *inukshuk*.

Kivitoo is an old whaling station, a spot discovered by whalers in 1925. There they established a camp and the equipment needed to melt whale blubber into oil. Some cauldrons remain visible. In the 1950s, Kivitoo served as a radar station, providing work for inhabitants of the nearby camps.

Padloping Island contains a traditional village where many of the residents of Broughton Island were born.

Reid Bay has been proposed as a bird sanctuary that would provide habitat for five major colonies of birds.

RECOMMENDATIONS

During your stay, you must function completely independently. You must register at Pangnirtung Park upon your arrival and departure. It is forbidden to take out any sort of samples or mementos or to leave any trace of your stay, such as trash or papers. To contribute to the overall knowledge of the park, write your observations (movement of animals and identification of rare flowers, for example) and tell park officials what you have seen.

The Inuit civilization was hit full force by the arrival of Europeans in the nineteenth century. Baffin Land remains a special place to meet Inuit who have been able to blend the European influence with the heritage of thousands of years of life in the north. That is why you must show the greatest respect for the native people that you will meet.

Nowadays, the Inuit are increasingly confined to reserves. They once led nomadic lives in one of the most hostile environments on earth. Forced to abandon their hunting camps and native ways by the influences of outsiders, they had to settle in permanent communities where their old values and beliefs were all but eroded.

109

peoples of the north, including the Inuit, Finns, Samoyeds, and Chukchis.

The survival of the Inuit in these polar regions is based equally on the hunting of seals, the narwhal, and the walrus. The population of northern right whales, estimated at 11,000 when their exploitation began, was not more than 300 when the hunt ended in 1913. That whale is listed as an endangered species.

In the raptor category, the gyrfalcon, peregrine falcon, and snowy owl share the tundra. To the north of Broughton Island, Cape Searly welcomes 200,000 pairs of fulmars. For the Inuit, the fulmar is the "whale bird" because it follows the krill that float to the surface when a whale is feeding. Around Kekerten Island, it is possible to view the right whale, caribou, polar bears, eider ducks, and black guillemot.

Observation

The polar bear feeds mainly on seals and, to locate its prey, spends most of its time on the ice or along the coast, following the ice chunks that drift off the north and east coasts of Baffin Island. That is why it is rare to see the bear in the Pangnirtung Pass. However, females give birth on the east coast of Baffin Land, so you can see them in the interior of the park after they leave their dens around April.

Those who travel and camp must be very vigilant with the bears. It is not rare to be awakened in the middle of the night by a bear that has come to prowl around the tent, attracted by the smell of camp food that may spread far. Usually a gunshot in the air will drive it away, but it is dangerous to remain two nights in the same place because the bear may return the second night. The solution is to sleep aboard a boat to avoid having to kill a too-curious bear. The Inuit hunt seals and, just after a capture, they cut up the animal on shore. This is the surest way to attract polar bears, which feed on seal fat. But the Inuit are protected by their dogs, who warn them of danger.

The risks are higher in the summer, when it is most difficult for the bears to catch seals. Moreover, at this time the young have just left their mothers and are on their own for the first time with no experience. They have difficulty finding nourishment and, not yet having developed a fear of humans, approach inhabited places more readily. One must be equally careful with a mother accompanied by a year-old cub.

Try to avoid surprise encounters with the bears by being aware of your surroundings. If you see a polar bear in the distance, don't attract its attention. If it starts to approach, never run away. Either walk slowly or if you can force yourself, play dead.

110

As everywhere in its range, the polar bear is forced to move onto dry land in summer. In Baffin Land, this period lasts only one month and a half.

Norway: Svalbard archipelago

Spitzbergen, located between 74 and 81 degrees north latitude, is almost halfway between the North Cape of Norway, which is 398 miles (637 km) from its southernmost point, and the North Pole, which is 626 miles (1,020 km) from its northernmost point. Sixty percent of the island is covered by ice, with the longest glacial surface measuring 125 miles (200 km). The ice floes follow the cold water currents, one of which comes from the pole and moves to the west, and two others that move along the east coast. One reverse warm current, the Gulf Stream, flows along the west coast, giving it a relatively mild climate for the latitude and freeing the sea of ice in the summer. Although it is probable that the archipelago was visited by Vikings about the year 1000, it was only at the end of the sixteenth century that history records explorers

officially landing there. In 1596 the explorer Willem Barents recorded the presence of a bear on the island now called the Isle of Bears (74 degrees 30' N) to the far south of Spitzbergen, the main island of Svalbard. A short time later, because of its proximity to Europe, the archipelago suffered the attacks of trappers and whale and seal hunters. The bears, attracted by the beached whales and walrus carcasses, paid a heavy tribute to the men, as is attested sadly by shipboard records.

During the centuries that followed, repeated expeditions reached the archipelago. The adventurers used floating wood, brought from Siberia by the transpolar current, to serve as building materials and fuel. In the twentieth century, all parts of the archipelago were explored: the peaks were climbed, points of departure for the North Pole were established, and men crossed the archipelago. All available means were used: by foot, on skis, in vehicles, in kayaks, and in balloons. Little by little, tourism also developed.

Svalbard has been under Norwegian rule since 1920. The bears have been protected by royal decree since 1978. Their population has increased since then, and it is believed essential to take measures to prevent any sort of indicent during a visit to a place where the bear reigns.

111

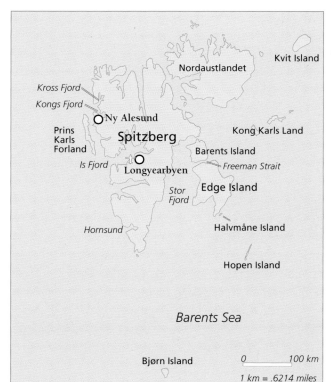

Kross Fjord
Kongs Fjord
Ny Alesund
Prins Karls Forland
Spitzberg
Is Fjord
Longyearbyen
Nordaustlandet
Kvit Island
Kong Karls Land
Barents Island
Freeman Strait
Stor Fjord
Edge Island
Hornsund
Halvmåne Island
Hopen Island

Barents Sea

Bjørn Island

0 _____ 100 km
1 km = .6214 miles

Flora and fauna

In the winter, some animals such as the arctic fox and the ivory gull follow closely the movements of the bears because they take advantage of what the bear leaves behind. Together with the ptarmigan, these are the only animals that remain all winter on Spitzbergen.

The beginning of summer is a time of intense activity; when the flowers, warmed by the first rays of sun, begin to come up under the snow, many seabirds come to nest during the short arctic summer. The kittiwakes and Brunnich's and Troil's guillemots find spots along the heights of the cliffs; lower down, their principal predator, the glaucous gull, establishes its nest. A bit farther away, black guillemots and puffins dig their burrows in a grassy slope. Little auks invade the fallen rocks. In the carpet of flowers, snow buntings and purple sandpipers conceal themselves. Long-tailed, pomarine, arctic, and great skuas watch visitors who are too curious and reject them with a flick of the wing. The strident cries of the arctic terns resound on the lake shores, and those of the red-throated loon sound like a wail of distress. Eiders and pink-footed geese fly along the shoreline. Among the marine mammals, seals rest on the icebergs close to the glacier walls. The once-abundant walrus is just now beginning to repopulate the archipelago. Reindeer and arctic fox are the only species of land mammal.

One hundred sixty-four species of flower live in the scarce ice-free spaces. Very

112

Moss campion and lichens form little islands to give them better resistance to the arctic climate; squeezed one against the other, their leaves form a microclimate.

In the summer, the ptarmigan and its covey hide among the rocks. In the autumn, its plumage is as white as the snow.

sensitive to the slightest variation in climate (amount of snow, wind, and soil moisture), they proliferate near colonies of birds and inhabited areas. They begin to grow under the snow, then sometimes flower for only a few days after the snow has melted. Saxifrages, arctic eriophorum, and arctic arnica form very colorful carpets in July. In August the dwarf willow sets the tone with its red coloration.

Observation

The west coast of Spitzbergen is bathed by the warm waters of the Gulf Stream. There the ice breaks up early, forcing the bears to make seasonal moves to stay in contact with the areas richest in seals, especially mottled seals.

Observation has shown that a certain number of bears migrate across the glaciers, passing from Horsund in the southwest to the Stor Fjord in the northeast at the end of winter and the beginning of spring. Thus,

they end up on the east coast, which is still very icebound in the summer. Other routes, such as the Freeman Strait between the Edge and Barents Islands, are also used often.

Surely the best time to see the bears is in the summer, when the diminution of sea ice concentrates them in the east. Observers may use several approaches to these sites. Hiking conditions are not the best: the soft underfooting makes progress slow, and the route is at times blocked abruptly by a fjord, glacier, or river. Added to this is the difficulty of walking with a loaded backpack. In contrast, a sailboat provides great freedom and a good chance of seeing a bear on the shore or bathing. Also, this mode reduces the risks of confrontation. A kayak is an ideal mode of transportation for moving through the fjords and along the coast at close range. However, visitors must take normal precautions in setting up camp.

The polar bear is completely protected and is reproducing well. The population reached its nadir in the 1970s, and it seems to be making a very visible comeback. Today the size is estimated at between 1,700 and

113

On the east coast, campgrounds may be visited by bears attracted by human waste. That is why it is better to avoid storing food inside the tent.

2,200 individuals. Long absent from the western part of the archipelago, the bear now seems to be colonizing that part of the region. Sightings in the region of King's Bay (Kongs Fjord) and Kross Fjord are more and more frequent. King Charles Land (Kong Karls Land, 78 degrees 55' N), located in the extreme east of the archipelago, is one of the three largest zones of polar bear reproduction in the world. It is in Boggen Valley that pregnant females find favorable conditions of snow cover, but most of all of quiet, far from the constant passage of trappers, to establish their dens. Ninety percent of these shelters are located among King Charles Land and the Edge, Barents, and Nordauslandet Islands. Females who give birth at these sites inhabit Svalbard, but they also live in northwestern Siberia. Other dens are scattered over the archipelago, on Hopen Island, the Isle of Bears, and in the northwestern part of Spitzbergen.

The purple sandpiper blends perfectly with tundra vegetation. Thinking itself invisible, the bird allows an approach to within a few meters.

The last voyage of Willem Barents

It was to correct a navigational error that the Dutchman Willem Barents sailed his ship into the waters of Svalbard in the sixteenth century. Sent for the third time by the council of the city of Amsterdam to discover the Northwest Passage to China, Barents went to sea in 1596 and did not return from the journey. We have information about the expedition from the accounts of several writers, among them the well-known Gerrit de Veer. Let us take up part of the story, dated June 12: "They saw a white bear and sent the rowboat toward it to try to get a large snare around it and hit it. However, they did not dare to take it on because it was quite furious. As they were hitting it, one sailor succeeded in burying his hatchet in the bear's back. He could not pull it out, and the bear carried him out into the water. Its skin was twelve feet long. They ate its meat, but they did not find it tasty. This incident caused them to name this island Beeren Eylandt, or Isle of the Bears." (Excerpt from *Prisonniers des glaces*, Editions Chandeign, 1996.) The result of the expedition was a succession of confrontations between hunters and bears. The combination of adventures multiplied the epic tales of hand-to-hand combat, of blows from halberds or fatal bites. On September 15, 1596, the navigators found themselves on the Coast of Novaya Zemlya: "The other bear remained as if astonished; it stared at its companion stretched out on the ground, and, seeing it make no movement at all, finally sniffed it and left. We watched it, and when we saw it coming back and standing up on its hind legs to attack the sailors, we delivered a shot to its stomach, which made it come down onto all four feet and flee, letting out great cries. We opened up the dead bear, and, after cutting out its entrails, we set it up on its four feet and left it to freeze in that position, with the intention of taking it back to Holland if we had the good fortune to release our ship from the ice." These stories, rendered in realistic images by the engravings of Theodore De Bry, contributed greatly to eliminating the idea of a sanguinary, terrifying polar bear.

PRACTICAL INFORMATION

The best time to observe the bears in Spitzbergen is summer,
when the melting of the ice forces them to concentrate in the east.

TRANSPORTATION

■ **BY AIR.** A flight connects Oslo with Longyearbyen, capital of Spitzbergen, with a stopover at Tromsø in northern Norway. At Spitzbergen you can charter a plane for Ny Alesund or Sveagruva; a helicopter can land you anywhere if the weather is suitable.

■ **BY BOAT.** You can rent a Zodiac to pass through the fjords in the vicinity of Longyearbyen. Small boats go to the north two or three times per week from Longyearbyen to Ny Alesund. You can also land farther north.

■ **BY CAR.** There are few road networks, and they are located only around the capital. It is best to rent a car to go between your lodging and stores to buy clothing and stock up on food dehydrated for a summer stay.

LODGING

A hotel, a youth hostel, and a campground near the Longyearbyen Airport are the only places that provide accommodations for outsiders. The campground offers facilities with kitchens, common rooms, showers, and lavatories, which are open from mid-June to the end of August. Elsewhere on the archipelago, only camping is possible.

Numerous shelters are scattered along the coast; they are private property and can only be used in case of emergency. Some of them are stocked with medications, dehydrated food, and, occasionally, an observation notebook for visitors to fill out.

CLIMATE

The summers in Spitzbergen are relatively mild, 39 to 41 degrees F (4 to 5 degrees C), and fog is frequent near the coasts. Violent storms can surprise travelers, even in the summer.

The first snowfalls come at the end of August. The permanently frozen soil unfreezes to a depth of 19.7 inches (50 cm) to 79 inches (2 m) in the summer, allowing plants to grow. In the winter, January through March are the coldest months, averaging 12 degrees F (−11 degrees C).

PLACES TO VISIT

At Ny Alesund, a bust of Roald Amundsen recalls the flight he made to the pole in a dirigible in 1926. A small museum traces the history of the village.

Old bear traps are partly visible throughout the archipelago, with an especially notable one at Ny Alesund. The bear, attracted by a piece of meat, would trigger a gun connected by a string to the bait and receive a bullet directly in the head.

The Museum in Longyearbyen displays various models of traps. One stuffed specimen of a polar bear gives an idea of how large the species is. The museum also presents the history of Spitzbergen and the exploitation of minerals and other natural resources. A small store offers maps and books. Spitzbergen is one of the rare places in the world where one climbs upward to mine coal. The deposits run horizontally at a higher altitude, and are quite thin. Most of the mines are closed today. At Longyearbyen, the wagons that brought out the coal were suspended from cables; they have been brought out and displayed for their historical interest. Coal mining is not profitable, but it continues for strategic reasons because of the presence of the Russians. The area around the town of Longyearbyen is blackened by coal dust.

RECOMMENDATIONS

Tourism in Spitzbergen is highly regulated: the governor (*Sysselman,* in Norwegian) requires of every group that goes outside inhabited regions to pay a deposit to cover the cost of searching for them in case of a problem. If the deposit is not paid, he himself decides on an amount to be paid in case expenses are incurred. The other regulations are the same as those in the rest of Norway. Regulations concerning the polar bear are very strict. Killing a bear is permissible only in self-defense, and the killer must submit proof to the authorities, with a narrative, sketch, and autopsy of the bear that was killed. The skin and the carcass remain the property of the Norwegian government. Between 1987 and 1992, 26 animals were killed under these circumstances. Encounters with bears are more and more frequent, and it is necessary to arm yourself with a large-caliber (a minimum of 7 millimeters) firearm as well as firecrackers in case of a face-to-face encounter while hiking or skiing.

Hiking requires some precautions, especially when traversing rivers and approaching moraines. On small boats, you must avoid approaching icebergs and glacier walls.

115

APPENDIX

Living with bears

Bears are like people: most of them are tolerant and sociable, but some are cantankerous and irascible. Some situations put bears under stress that makes them dangerous: the rutting season for males, and the presence of young cubs for females, as well as wounds or a history of hostile contact with people.

Wise Precautions

In all situations, the bear must not identify a person as a potential source of food. Some advice is necessary to avoid dangerous contact:

• Never carry fresh food in your backpack.
• Never fry fish or bacon near your encampment, to avoid impregnating your tent with food odors.
• In American and Canadian parks, use the special trash receptacles to deposit your trash. If these are not available, burn the trash and carry out anything that remains.
• Do not keep food in your tent.
• Do not keep toothpaste, soap, or other perfumed items in your tent.
• Do not brush your teeth in rivers, lest the river carry away an odor that may attract bears.
• Tents must be pitched sufficiently far apart so that a bear can pass between them.
• **Young children and menstruating women should not be present at campsites.**

Hunters and trappers are most often attacked: clothing soaked with blood, greasy hands, game carcasses, and entrails attract bears. When you move around, you must avoid surprising a bear, and it is preferable that they detect your presence first. Give

them a signal with a bell, talk or sing when crossing areas with low visibility, thickets, or dense forests that are likely to attract bears, as well as bushes where berries grow in abundance. Avoid walking into the wind. If you notice a young bear alone, do not go near it—its mother is not far, and a bear in that situation is the most dangerous kind.

If you find a deer carcass in a forested area with large numbers of bears, leave the area quickly—don't become a possible competitor for the bear. When camping in the wild, choose a site far from loud streams

American national parks offer the visitor containers for storing food, to avoid attracting bears to their tents.

and from indications that bears have been present (droppings, tracks, scratches).

Signs of Aggressiveness

Although the behavior of bears is largely determined by the situation, it is possible to make a list of the attitudes and postures that do or do not indicate that aggressiveness, always remembering that every situation is unique.

• **The bear is standing on its hind legs:** this is not a position of aggression. The bear is seeking olfactory and visual information.

118

Double page preceding. Grizzly bears are good swimmers, they swim across lakes and ponds. During the summer, they like to swim on hot days.

• **The bear takes a side position**: it is presenting its profile to a human to impress the human with its size. Upon meeting another bear, this position might be one of appeasement.
• **The bear faces you**: this is an aggressive attitude, and the animal expects you to back away.
• **The bear snorts**: if it is tense, it may emit a series of sharp, harsh snorts.
• **The bear emits a "woof"**: if a young bear emits this sound, it puts the mother on alert immediately.
• **The bear clicks its jaws**: it is nervous and stressed. A female warns her young of danger in this way.
• **Roars, grunts, and growls**: strong indication of intolerance.
• **Unusual salivation**: a clear sign of tension.
• **Charge**: an aggressive or defensive attitude. Most often, it is a charge done to intimidate. The bear may or may not emit vocal sounds before charging.

Although the precautions described above are usually enough for the grizzly bear and the black bear, they are not adequate in dealing with polar bears. A large-caliber gun is required for moving around in Spitzbergen, Churchill, and Baffin Land. Since Spitzbergen's regulations permit every visitor to carry a firearm, it is wise to take advantage of the provision. A gun of too small a caliber could cost you your life (there was one such death in Spitzbergen in 1995). It is also necessary to know your gun well and to have it tested and maintained regularly.

In Manitoba and in the Northwest Territories, it is better to use the services of a guide who can ensure the security of your group. Recently, the sale of aerosol cans loaded with a red-colored material has been permitted on the open market. (However, carrying such protection on airplanes is prohibited.) These systems have saved the lives of many hunters and hikers who have encountered grizzlies. An extreme emergency protection effective only at close range (16.4 feet [5 m], or closer), the aerosols require care when used; for example, you must not spray them into the wind. They are recommended for use in the forest. Emergency flares and Bengal lights are also efficient and inexpensive individual means of protection that are easy to use.

Observing and photographing bears

To see a bear in the wild is a dream that many nature lovers share. The symbol of wildlife in the forests of the Northern Hemisphere, the bear is a "must" in the same category as the large whales and the large raptors. Some regions allow discovery of bears in excellent conditions, as we have seen.

Before any visit to a bear observation site, you first must be acquainted with the way of life of the species present. Park employees will be quite ready to furnish information on

The area around Churchill is marked with signs giving a very clear impression of the risks; going farther could be dangerous.

the daily and spatial habits of the bears in their jurisdiction. An awareness of the signs of its presence will alert the visitor and lead to other useful observations. The contents and freshness of droppings indicate the bear's present diet and the type of vegetation it prefers. If a bear has just run away, and you did not have the opportunity to see it, it very likely defecated under the stress of the surprise meeting.

One of the best ways to see grizzlies is to wait in a place that has been marked, after having studied the spot thoroughly. The

119

bears are unadventurous and pass often through the same areas, as is proven by the distinct trails they leave through high grass and their repeated tracks. Along the shore, low tide is the time the bears choose to walk along the beach in search of a crab, a dead fish, or the carcass of a marine mammal. In the summer they frequent ponds in the middle of the day to cool off. Dumps are always easy sites to observe and photograph bears, although some dumps have been made bear-proof. At the dumps visitors have an opportunity to get an idea of the bear's animal nature, but in no way is a bear stuffed with human food an indication of its behavior in the wild.

Photography

Articles and books that contain many magnificent photographs of bears might give the impression that this activity is easy. All of those images come from known sites, most of which are described in this book. The shooting there is often easy, the bears numerous, the conditions for observation ideal, and the photographers are often **120** specialists in large predators.

Precautions

In no case should a photographer follow a bear, because the bear might feel threatened and turn to face its pursuer.

If you are waiting to observe or photograph a bear, do not make an exaggerated effort to hide, because the bear can sense your presence before you see the bear, and you risk being approached and surprised.

Do not use a hunting blind. Bears are incredibly quiet. Even in dense forests, they move soundlessly, without stirring the smallest branch. Always be looking around you. In a group of photographers, one person must be assigned to be in charge of security. The field of a blind limits your visual range considerably, and the excitement of a sighting may cause you to forget the most rudimentary precautions.

The photographer must not be deceived by the placidity of the subject and so approach too closely. Bear behavior is unpredictable; in some places American black bears, reputed to be a tolerant species, will come to eat out of a person's hand, others will make deliberate attacks.

Do not venture into a riverbed, because that is the bears' fishing territory.

Advice

People and bears can cohabit quite successfully if the observers remain outside the realm of the bears' activity. This relationship is best seen in McNeil River and Brooks Camp, where photographers, fishermen, and grizzlies have spent their days in harmony for dozens of years without a single incident.

At Churchill, shooting pictures is usually an important part of the trip. For a 35-mm camera, the lens may be from 80 to 200 mm for close shots (the focal distance used most when bears are abundant) and 400 mm for long-range shots at the beginning of the migratory period.

A monopod is not essential, but is recommended. If you do not bring one, use a "beanbag" on which to rest the camera in the truck window. Black-and-white film should not be neglected because it gives outstanding results in overcast weather. When taking color photographs, be careful to use a film that is sufficiently neutral. Avoid film that is too dull, because it will destroy contrast and shadows.

In most cases, at the end of October the sky is overcast and gray, but it reflects light. If you are lucky, the sun may appear. For the possible aurora borealis, bring a light-sensitive film and use a technique similar to that used when taking pictures of stars and planets. Bring optical components with an aperture of 2.8 or more, a tripod, a flexible shutter release, and a camera with a B position.

Protecting bears

Although international cooperation has succeeded fully in protecting such symbols as the polar bear, populations of other species that are less well known and occupy less progressive countries are declining dangerously fast. The giant panda is isolated in pockets that are shrinking like patches of spring snow, encircled by an ever-growing human population. Poaching, despite the threat of heavy punishment, is still practiced. The original habitat of the Asiatic tropical bears has been reduced by 67 percent since 1900.

The Asiatic black bear has been accused of attacking domestic animals and damaging trees, such as oaks, cherries, dogwoods, and beeches. In Japan it attacks cypress and cedar trees, species with considerable value. Every year some 3,000 bears are killed for this reason. They have disappeared from some parts of Japan, Pakistan, and Korea.

The sun bear, smallest of the bears, is the least-studied species, although it is a popular animal in Thailand. Large parts of its habitat continue to be destroyed by cultivation, cutting of forests, and establishment of farms. It is sold in Thai markets and ends up at the end of a leash. The sloth bear is in direct competition with the villagers of India because of its strong attraction for a particular flower, the mohwa, which blooms in the spring and which villagers ferment to produce an alcoholic beverage. It is also suffering from the population explosion on the Indian subcontinent in the forests of India and Sri Lanka. A timid animal, it cannot stand the proximity of people and has taken refuge in some regions that remain uninhabited.

South America faces problems even more significant than those in Asia. Bears are especially vulnerable in the face of alteration or loss of their habitat. Their diet forces them to move long distances and to share food resources. Habitat destruction has isolated small groups of bears. This isolation limits genetic exchange among individuals and increases the risk of inbreeding, which is harmful to the health of a species. The proximity of human settlements pushes bears to seek food in planted fields, orchards, and even in vegetable gardens and dumps. They attack beehives and domestic animals that they can capture easily. Farmers and foresters who consider them a menace continue to kill them, even when the species is protected by international law; the law is very difficult to enforce in such locations.

In countries where no subsidies are given for the study of bears, data on the populations and their behavior is nonexistent. In that case, sometimes inappropriate conservation measures are taken.

Other reports add to this black picture. In Peru, the spectacled bear is widely hunted for sport and for its meat, which reportedly

The Abruzzi Park has established a program to study bears. The guards wear the park emblem, the Marsican bear.

is excellent, as well as for its fur and its fat. Local natives capture it for sale to rich Venezuelans and Colombians seeking an unusual pet.

Despite warning cries from various international organizations such as the World Wildlife Fund, CITES (Convention on International Trade in Endangered Species of Flora and Fauna), and the IUCN (International Union for the Conservation of Nature and Natural Resources), constant destruction of habitat of these species continues. Research programs are not part of

121

the priorities of the governments in question. In China, some 10,000 bears are kept in captivity for the extraction of their bile, under the pretext of sparing wild animals. However, these individuals will never be released. This livestock farming only perpetuates the medicinal traditions and prevents research for new remedies.

In Nepal, the Chitwan National Park, established twenty years ago, has taken positive action for the protection of the tiger. At the same time, the sloth bear population has done so well that in 1990 a research program for tracking them by radio was judged to have accomplished its goal. This was the first in-depth attempt to study this species.

The spectacled bear has the advantage of a mountainous habitat that gives it provisional shelter. But if it is to survive, natural corridors must be maintained among isolated populations to allow them to reproduce. In many regions of Southeast Asia, children consider bear cubs as domestic animals. Once they grow to adulthood, they are sold on the black market for their bile. If no expert comes to educate the population about the urgency of protecting these species, these habits that have been fixed in people's minds for centuries will endure until the bear has become extinct.

Conservation of Species

The IUCN has established two lists that divide bears according to the potential risk of a species disappearing:

Vulnerable: a threatened species that could be in danger of extinction in the near future if unfavorable factors are not ended shortly.

Endangered: a species in danger of extinction, whose survival is unlikely if the cause of its disappearance persists.

The CITES categorizes species to regulate trade and transport of entire animals or parts of animals and plants.

Appendix I: Rare or endangered species in which trade for commercial purposes is not permitted. Permits for transport and capture can be granted for scientific purposes.

Appendix II: Species that are not rare or endangered but that may become so if traffic in them is not regulated. An export permit is required when removing them from the country.

	CITES	IUCN red book
PANDA	Appendix I	endangered
SPECTACLED BEAR	Appendix I	endangered
SUN BEAR	Appendix I	endangered
SLOTH BEAR	Appendix I	endangered
ASIATIC BLACK BEAR	Appendix I	vulnerable
NORTH AMERICAN BLACK BEAR	Appendix II	not classified
GRIZZLY BEAR Species in Bhutan, China, Mexico, and Mongolia and the supspecies U.a.isabellinus (India and Pakistan)	Appendix I	not classified
Other populations and subspecies	Appendix II	
POLAR BEAR	Appendix II	vulnerable

In addition to the international classifications, each signatory country of the Washington Convention can enforce protection measures and import and export conditions for products derived from plantigrades. For example, the United States prohibits the import of polar bear skins, even with a CITES certificate. France prohibits all transport and handling of the grizzly bear on its territory.

Some associations and organizations involved with bears

In France
Artus BP 39
41003 Blois CEDEX

Fonds d'Intervention Eco-Pastoral
groupe Ours BP 508
64010 PAU UNIVERSITE CEDEX

Société Française d'Etude et de Protection
des Mammifères, groupe Ours
c/o Service du Patrimoine naturel M.N.H.N.
57, rue Cuvier
75231 Paris CEDEX 05

In Belgium
Groupe Ours RNOB
105, rue Royale Sainte-Marie
1040 Bruxelles

In Spain
Foundation Oso-Pardo,
rue Isabelle la Catholique 7/4
39007 Santander

In Greece
Arcturos 3, Aghiou Mina str.
546 25 Thessaloniki
Concerned with protecting trained bears

In the United States
Craighead Wildlife Wildlands Institute, 5
200 Upper Miller Creek Road
Missoula, Montana 59803

Great Bear Foundation,
PO Box 1289
Bozeman, Montana 59715

Great Yellowstone Coalition
PO Box 1874
Bozeman, Montana 59715

Yellowstone Grizzly Foundation
581 Expedition Drive
Evanstone, Wyoming 82930

Denali Foundation Grizzly Foundation
Box 212
Denali Park, Alaska 99755

North American Bear Society
3875 North 44th St., suite 102
Phoenix, Arizona 85018

In Canada
Valhalla Wilderness Society
Box 329
New Denver, British Columbia V0G 1S0

Grizzly Project
PO Box 957
Nelson, British Columbia VIL 6A5

123

Dictionary

English	French	Russian	Norwegian
annual cycle	cycle annuel	yezhegodnyi tsikl	ars syklus
ant	fourmi	muravey	maur
bear	ours	medved'	bjorn
bear trainer	montreur d'ours	voyak medvedya	bjorneguide
bedding site	couche	logovo	soveplass
berry	baie	yagoda	baer
caribou	caribou	kariby	reinsdyr
carrion	charogne	mertvechina	kadaver
cinnamon	cannelle	koritsa	kanel
claw	griffe	kogot'	klu
coat (of an animal)	fourrure	mekh	pels
cub	ourson	medvezhonok	unge
den	tanière	berloga	hi
dump	décharge	naval	kaste, dumpe
fasting	jeune	golodavka	faste
front paw	patte avant	perednyaya lapa	framlabb
hair	poil	sherst'	har
hind paw	patte arrière	zadnyaya lapa	baklabb
ice pack	banquise	toros	pakkis
litter, garbage	poubelle	musor	soppel
marking	indice	sled	a merke
moose	élan	los'	elg
nursing	allaitement	kormlenie	pleie
omnivorous	omnivore	vseyadnyy	altetere
plantigrade	plantigrade	stopokhodyashchiy	helgaer
poaching	braconnage	brakon'yerstvo	tjuvjakte
prey	proie	dobycha	bytte
range	répartition	raspredelenie	revir
root	racine	koren'	rot
safety	sécurité	bezopasnost'	sikkerhet
salmon	saumon	losos'	laks
scat, droppings	crotte, fèces	pomet	mo
scratch	griffade	udar kogtyami	kloremerker
seal	phoque	tyulen'	sel
spawning area	zone de ponte (poisson)	nerestilshche	lekeplassice floe,
teeth	denture	zuby	tannstilling
thicket	fourre	chashcha	busk
to amble	aller l'amble	bezhat' inokhod' yu	spasere
to dig	creuser	ryt'	agrave
to growl	grogner	vortchat'	brole, grymte
to make noise	faire du bruit	shumet'	brake
to pop the jaws	claquer les mâchoires	stychat' zubami	gap
to surprise	surprendre	zastat' vrasplokh	overraske
toes	doigts	pal'tsy	taer
track	piste	sledy	spor
track	trace	sled	svtrykk
trap	piège	lovushka	felle
unpredictable	imprévisible	neozhidanno	uforutsigbar
wintering	hivernage	zimovka	vinteraktig
young	juvenile	yunyy	arsunge

Glossary

Amble: pace of a quadruped that moves both feet on the same side of its body at the same time in each step

Amerindian: term for all peoples native to America

Cambium: tender layer under the bark that is the source of a tree's growth

Chitin: solid material forming the exoskeleton of insects

Color phase: referring to a group of individuals of a species that has more than one color

Dimorphism, sexual: obvious morphological difference between the sexes of a species

Estrus: period of receptivity to mating of a female

Faunistic: having to do with fauna

Feces: synonym for scat or droppings

Floristic: having to do with flora

Glabrous: referring to a hairless skin

Gravid: synonym for pregnant

Gregarious: referring to a species that lives in groups

Hibernation: process of slowed life functions that permits the winter survival of some species

Myrmeco-: prefix referring to ants

Phylogeny: succession of phases in the evolution of a species

Phylum: genealogical branch in the evolution of a group of species

Plantar Surface: part of the foot that comes in contact with the ground

Plantigrade: mammal that places its entire foot surface on the ground with each step

Polynya: area of open water in an ice floe, kept open by currents

Protocol: assembly of rules to be followed during a ceremony

Same: people of Finno-Ugric descent, more commonly called Lapps

Spermophile: rodent that digs a burrow in the ground and feeds mainly on seeds

Taiga: northern conifer forest

Tundra: low vegetation composed of mosses and plants typical of polar regions

Wean: to stop nursing the young

Bibliography

General works

Barbeau, M., *Totem Poles, According to Crest and Topics.* Canadian Museum of Civilization, 1990.

Clarkson, P. L., *Safety in Bear Country.* Department of Renewable Resources, Northwest Territories, 1986.

Herrero, S., *Bear Attacks: Their Causes and Avoidance.* Piscataway, New Jersey, Winchester Press, 1985.

Lajoux, J.-D. *L'Homme et l'Ours.* Glénat, 1996.

Marion, R. and J.-P. Sylvestre, *Guide des Phoques, Otaries et Siréniens.* Delachaux et Niestlé, 1993.

Praneuf, M., *L'Ours et les hommes.* Imago, 1989.

Robbins, Chandler S., Bertel Bruun, and Herbert S. Zim, *Guide des Oiseaux d'Amérique du Nord.* Delachaux and Niestlé, 1980.

Rockwell, D., *Giving Voice to Bears.* Roberts Rinehart, 1991.

Stewart, H., *Looking at Totem Poles.* Douglas and McIntyre, 1993.

Stirling, I., editor, *Bears: Majestic Creatures of the Wild.* Rodale Press, 1993.

Stroganov, S. U., *Carnivorous Mammals of Siberia.* Academy of Sciences of the USSR, Israeli Program for Scientific Translations, 1969.

Vaisfield, M. A. and I. E. Chestin, eds. *Bears, Game Animals of Russia and Adjacent Countries and Their Environment.* Moscow, Nauka, 1993.

Ward, P. and S. Kynaston, *Bears of the World.* Blandford Books, 1995.

Books to bring with you

IN ALASKA AND CANADA:

Alaska and Yukon Wild Flowers Guide. Alaska Northwest, 1974.

Field Guide of the Birds of North America. National Geographic Society, 1987.

Olsen, L., *Field Guide to the Grizzly Bear: Understanding and Safety in Western North America.* Sasquatch Books, 1992.

Whitaker, John O., *The Audubon Society Field Guide to North American Mammals.* New York: Alfred A. Knopf, 1980.

IN RUSSIA:

Flint, V. E., R. L. Boehme, Y. V. Kostin, and A. A. Kuznetsov, *A Field Guide to Birds of the USSR.* Princeton, 1984.

125

Johnson, L., *Guide des Oiseaux de l'Europe*. Nathan, 1994.

Russia, Ukraine, and Belarus. Lonely Planet, 1996.

IN BULGARIA AND ITALY:

En Bulgarie. Guides VISA, Hachette, 1995.

Peterson, R., G. Mountfort, P .A. D. Hollom, and P. Geroudet, *Guide des Oiseaux de France et d'Europe*. Delachaux et Niestlé, 1994.

IN NORWAY (SVALBARD):

Bodineau, G. *Spitzberg, l'Archipel de Svalbard*. GNGL Travel Books DMI, 1994.

De Veer, G. *Prisonniers des Glaces: Les Expéditions de Willem Barentsz (1594–1597)*, introduction by Xavier de Castro. Chandeigne/UNESCO, 1996.

Black bear

Anderson, T. *Black Bear: Seasons in the Wild*. Voyager Press, 1992.

Bacon, E. S. "Curiosity in the American Black Bear," Fourth International Conference on Bear Research and Management. Kalispell Mountain Bear Biology Association Conference Series no. 4, 153–57, 1977.

Jenkins, K. L., *Black Bear Reflections*. ICS Books, 1995.

Jolicoeur, H. and R. Lemieux, *Quelques Aspects de la Reproduction de l'Ours Noir au Québec*. Ministry of Recreation, Hunting, and Fishing, Province of Québec, 1994.

Paquet, P., *Black Bear Ecology in the Riding Mountains*. Prepared for Manitoba Natural Resources Service and Canadian Park Service by John/Paul and Associates, 1991.

Grizzly bear

Camarra, J.-J., *L'Ours Brun*. Hatier Publications, 1989.

Couturier, M., *L'Ours Brun*. Published by author, 1954.

Craighead, J.-J., J. S. Sumner, and J.A. Mitchell, *The Grizzly Bears of Yellowstone*. Island Press, 1995.

Gastou, F. R., *Sur les Traces des Montreurs d'Ours des Pyrénées et d'ailleurs*. Loubatiéres, 1984.

Hoshino, M. *Grizzly*. Chronicle Books, 1987.

Murray, J., *Grizzly Bears*. Roberts Rinehart, 1995.

Parde, J.-M. and J.-J. Camarra, "L'Ours des Pyrénées (*Ursus arctos* Linnaeus, 1758)," *Encyclopédie des Carnivores de France*, v. 5. SFEPM, 1992.

Rautiainen, L. *Mina Bjornar*. Arcticmedia, 1995.

Polar bear

Kurten, B. "The Evolution of the Polar Bear (*Ursus maritimus*, Phipps)," Acta Zool. Fenn., 108, 1964.

Larsen, T., "Population Biology of the Polar Bear (*Ursus maritimus*) in the Svalbard Area," *Norsk Polarinstitut Skifter* no. 184, 1986.

Marion, R. "L'Ours Polaire dans les Relations des Voyages de Jacques Cartier à Jean-Baptiste Charcot," in *J.-B. Charcot et la Continuité des Missions Polaires Françaises*. Groupe Rhone-Alpes de l'UFPP, 1996.

Ovsyannikov, N., *Polar Bears: Living with the White Bear*. Raincoast Books, 1996.

Randa, V. *L'Ours Polaire et les Inuit*. SELAF, 1986.

Stirling, I., *Polar Bears*. FitzHenry and Whiteside, 1989.

Wiig, O., "Distribution of Polar Bears (*Ursus maritimus*) in the Svalbard Area," *Journal of Zoology*, 515–29, 1995.

Videos

Alaska Grizzlies. Alaska Video Postcard, 1993.

Ghost Bear. BBC, 1994 (dedicated to the Mount Kermode bear).

L'Ours Blanc, Roi de la Banquise. Survival/Canal+, 1984.

La Femme qui Eleva un Ours comme un Fils. Kid Cartoons, 1991 (animated Inuit legend, for children).

La Montagne aux Ours. Artus, 1991 (distributed by the Artus Association).

Les Ours Géants de l'Ile Kodiak. National Geographic Video, 1994.

Les Royaumes de l'Ours Russe. A2/BBC Enterprises, 1992.

Living Among Ice Bears. A Naturalist World, 1995.

The Biggest Bears. Skyriver Films, 1993 (for children).

The Great Bears of North America. Bush Productions, 1996.

For American cassettes other than those produced by the National Geographic Society, consult the Great Bear Foundation.

Geographic index

Abruzzi, 64–68
Alaska, 42, 78, 83
Apennines, 64
Appalachians, 52
Auyuittuq, 106–110
Baffin Land, 106, 119
Balkans, 69–72
British Columbia, 38, 42
Brooks Camp, 83, 87, 120
Broughton Island, 106, 109
Bulgaria, 69
Canada, 42, 47, 96, 101, 106
Cantabrian Mountains, 60
Churchill, 96–100, 119–120
Denali, 78–82
Fairbanks, 81
Fort Severn, 101
Gatlinburg, 52, 55
Great Smoky Mountains, 52–55
Hudson Bay, 96–97, 103
Hyder, 42–46
Iqaluit, 109
Italy, 64–68
James Bay, 101–105
Kamchatka, 58, 60
Katmai, 83–87
Kodiak, 58, 77, 83, 86
Koni, 73
Longyearbyen, 111, 114
Magadan, 73–77
Manitoba, 47, 96, 119
McNeil River, 83, 120
Misty Fjords, 42
Montana, 60
Mount McKinley, 78–82
North Carolina, 52
Northwest Territories, 119
Norway, 111
Ny Alesund, 111, 114
Okhotsk, 73
Ontario, 101
Pangnirtung, 106, 109, 110
Pescasseroli, 64, 67

Polar Bear Provincial Park, 101–102
Portland, 42
Prince Rupert, 45
Pyrenees, 66
Rhodopes, 69, 72
Riding Mountain, 47–51
Romania, 60
Russia, 73
Shelikof Strait, 83
Siberia, 60, 73
Slovenia, 60
Sofia, 69, 72
Spitzbergen, 111, 119
Stara Planina, 69, 71
Stewart, 42
Svalbard, 111–115
Sweden, 60
Tennessee, 52
Tongass, 42
Umbria, 64
United States, 42, 52, 78, 83
Vancouver, 45
Winnipeg, 47, 51, 99
Yellowstone, 20, 58, 86

General index

Abruzzi bear, 68
Aggressiveness, signs of, 118–119
Ailuropoda melanoleuca, 32–33
American black bear, 34–55, 122
Asiatic black bear, 24–25, 121–122
Associations, 123
Barents Sea, 111
Barents, Willem, 114
Baribal, 34–35, 119, 122
Brown bear, 56–87, 119, 122
Cherokee, 54–55
Chukchi, 93, 108, 110
CITES, 122
Classification, 10
Cree, 103

Evolution, 10–11
Feces, 41, 63, 119
Firearms, 21, 93, 119
Giant panda, 32–33, 121–122
Gitskan, 44
Grizzly, 44, 77, 80, 82, 119–120
Hunting, 21, 49–50, 85, 93, 103, 108
Inuit, 106, 108, 110
IUCN, 122
Longevity, 17, 30, 32, 38, 60, 92
Malaysian bear, 26–27
Marsican bear, 68
Nourishment, 16, 24, 26, 28, 30, 36, 38, 58–60, 68, 71–72, 77, 82, 86, 92, 110
Photography, 119–120
Polar bear, 88–115, 119, 121–122
Precautions, 118, 120
Protection of bears, 121–122
Reproduction, 14–16, 24, 26, 28, 30, 32, 40, 62, 94–95
Salmon, 40, 63, 74, 84, 86
Same, 20
Samoyed, 108, 110
Scratches, 63
Sheep, Dall, 80
Sloth bear, 28–29, 121–122
Social life, 14
Spectacled bear, 30–31, 121–122
Sun bear, 26–27, 121–122
Tracks, 41, 63, 95
Tremarctos ornatus, 30–31
Ursus americanus, 34–55
Ursus arctos, 56–87
Ursus arctos marsicanus, 68
Ursus malayanus, 26–27
Ursus maritimus, 88–115
Ursus thibetanus, 24–25
Ursus ursinus, 28–29
Whales, 93, 110
Winter sleep, 12, 40–41, 62
Wolves, 48, 65, 79
World Wildlife Fund, 121

127

Acknowledgments
We offer our warm gratitude to those who
have made it possible for us to assemble the
material necessary and to travel to gather
information about the bears: Stefan Haglund
(Sweden), Pat Rousseau (Manitoba), Diane
Rioux (New Brunswick), Colette Fontaine
(Manitoba), Jim Halfpenny (British
Columbia), Bill Rogoza (Ontario), Anne
Zobenmulher and Daniele Cordisco
(Embassy of Canada), Raitcho Gunchev
(Bulgaria), Pavel Simeonov and Valera
Zarodnyy (Russia), Romain Paillard
(Rencontre Découverte), and Boris Czerny
and the airline companies Canadian Airlines
and Lufthansa.

Produced with the cooperation of
Anne Cauquetoux
Stéphanie Houlvigue

Research for art editing
Rémy MARION

Sources of Illustrations
J.-J. ALCALAY (BIOS): p. 118
Y. AMAND: pp. 70 top, 70 bottom, 72
M. COSSEC: pp. 107 top, 107 bottom, 108
  bottom
O. GRUNEWALD: pp. 14, 79 top, 79
  bottom, 82, 84 top, 84 bottom, 85 top, 86,
  98 bottom
M. GUNTHER (BIOS): p. 71
P. HALLEY (STOCK IMAGE): pp. 102 top,
  102 bottom, 103, 104
E. KEMILA (PHO.N.E.): pp. 13, 15
C. and R. MARION: cover, pp. 6, 8–9, 16,
  17, 18–19, 20, 21, 34–35, 36, 39, 41 top,
  41 bottom, 43 top, 43 bottom, 45, 46, 48,
  49 top, 49 bottom, 50 top, 50 bottom, 51,
  56–57, 60–63, 74 top, 74 bottom, 77, 85
  bottom, 88–89, 92, 93, 94, 97, 98 top, 99,
  100, 108 top, 110, 112 top, 112 bottom,
  114 top, 114 bottom, 116–117, 119
MAYWALD (Wildlife Gm BIOS): p. 53
M. MELODIA: pp. 65 top, 65 bottom, 66, 68,
  121
M. PERREAU: p. 75
R. PETOCZ (WWF BIOS): pp. 22–23
M. ROBLIN: p. 113
STOCK IMAGE: p. 40
R. VALARCHER (BIOS): p. 80